ADVENTURES
IN MIND

A PERSONAL OBS[...]
WITH THE MOUNTAINS

ADVENTURES
IN MIND

Vertebrate Publishing, Sheffield
www.v-publishing.co.uk

ADVENTURES IN MIND — HEATHER DAWE

First published in 2013 by Vertebrate Publishing.

VERTEBRATE PUBLISHING

Crescent House, 228 Psalter Lane, Sheffield S11 8UT.

www.v-publishing.co.uk

This book is a work of non-fiction based on the life, experiences and recollections of Heather Dawe.
In some limited cases the names of people, places, dates and sequences or the detail of events have been
changed solely to protect the privacy of others. The author has stated to the publishers that, except in such
minor respects not affecting the substantial accuracy of the work, the contents of the book are true.

Photos: Dawe collection unless otherwise credited.

A CIP catalogue record for this book is available from the British Library.

ISBN: 978-1-906148-69-0 (Paperback)

ISBN: 978-1-906148-70-6 (Ebook)

Design and production by Rod Harrison — Vertebrate Graphics Ltd. — www.v-graphics.co.uk

Printed and bound in the UK by T.J. International Ltd, Padstow, Cornwall.

CONTENTS

FOREWORD

Running up on the Chevin on a winter's night in the wind and drizzle you don't expect to meet many people. Maybe the odd dog walker, or an occasional clandestine mountain biker, but it's not often you actually meet another runner. On one such evening, jogging along the track below Chevin Buttress, I passed a fellow shady figure out running in the dark. We half crossed, muttering a greeting, but then both stopped mid-stride as we recognised one another — it was Heather.

Linking up to run together for a few minutes, I asked her what she'd been up to recently. *'Oh, you know — I've been getting out a bit.'* Now, Heather is good because she trains hard — ridiculously hard at times, with a level of self discipline that I can only dream of — so I knew that this really meant: *'I've been getting out in the dark and rain every night for months, grinding out a vast number of miles. A bit.'*

In the time I've known her, she's gone from being a rebellious young student to an accomplished rock climber; a 'clueless rookie' to an elite mountain marathoner and from a 'beer-bike' owner to winner of the Three Peaks Cyclo-Cross race. This is not normal.

Having the determination to set yourself such big physical goals and then going about achieving them repeatedly requires a complex mix of motivations — some of them almost as extreme as the physical challenges themselves. A degree of self-motivation bordering on obsession is pretty much mandatory and having something like that running around inside your head all the time can be a difficult thing to manage and control, let alone understand.

Yet Heather manages these motivations and emotions as skillfully as she runs and races, while still holding down a busy job running a large team and looking after a young daughter.

Driving hundreds of miles on a Friday night, sleeping in the back of a car, getting up before dawn, running/skiing/riding up and down mountains for several hours, crossing the finish line exhausted, jumping straight into the car to drive home and then being jumped on by small children all afternoon. I know the routine well. She's very lucky to have such a loving and supportive partner as Aidan in this respect. Juggling work, family life and 'play time' is a never-ending challenge.

Starting out as a climber, Heather ran her first mountain marathon in 1996, completing the C course on the KIMM in the Galloway Hills with Ellen Wolfenden. In typical climber style, neither of them really knew what they were doing with a map and compass — so they just stumbled around in the mist and completed the course anyway, with a good deal of blisters and swearing.

Many other races — and navigational errors — followed, but gradually an ambition was born: complete the OMM Elite course. En-route there were many setbacks and moments of questioning and doubt, but, rather than give in, Heather just stepped back a little and planned another training strategy to improve and overcome. It took eleven years from failing to find the first control on successive races, to mastering compass bearings in the Brecon Beacons, to completing the LAMM Elite on Mull and finally the OMM Elite course three times, winning both mixed and female pair categories.

This book follows one person's journey, told through a life among mountains — a longing to escape from the mundane grind of jobs and everyday life, to the freedom of the natural world.

Along the way, Heather questions why she does it: the training, the pain, the failure and — eventually — the success. Through the pages of *Adventures in Mind* I've been inspired to ask many of my own questions, but most of all I've been inspired to get out my trainers, dust off the bike and just get out and do it — and you can't ask for better inspiration than that.

Al Powell. Otley, April 2013

PROLOGUE

Finished Business

The last descent off Pen-y-ghent and I can't let myself think it's in the bag. Anything could happen, take it easy, take no risks. Just get to the finish and win. The Three Peaks Cyclo-Cross. An amazing race in which you get to carry your bike up three big hills in God's own county of Yorkshire. My favourite race and I was hoping for seventh time lucky. I had been second three times and to be honest I was getting a bit fed up. I really wanted to win and was starting to think it would never happen. I trained harder, and tried to lose the negative feelings. On race day I went for it and won, taking twelve minutes off my previous best.

It felt good, great even. A beautiful day out in a stunning place that all came together; I finally got my name on the trophy. So, what's next? I'll line up again next September. I'll train hard again, try and win, get a faster time. Will it be the same as last time? Have I succeeded enough or is it that winning isn't everything?

The challenge and anticipation that pushes me to try harder. The obsessive urge to achieve. It's not all about winning. Why do I do it?

The Grand Raid Cristalp, an amazing race in the Swiss Alps. Great climbs, descents, singletrack and a perverse last climb up to the Pas de Lona, shouldering your bike up a long scree ascent at just under 3000 metres. If the altitude doesn't take your breath, the scenery will. It is truly beautiful.

Starting the last and longest climb. I knew it was bad when my jaw started to cramp. When my fingers went too I felt like crying, my whole body was aching. The temptation to retire, to turn around and roll back down to the valley was so very strong. This wasn't the first time I had done this race. I had finished it before so what did I have to prove? Maybe, if I slowed right down, I could get timed out?

I carried on and finished. Over an hour slower than my fastest time but my best because I did not stop.

The fear of failure. A monkey on my back, whispering sweet nothings — it doesn't matter, just forget it, it's only a bike ride after all. I think it's a bit more than that. We all have our demons, don't we? Why don't I listen, why can't I stop?

The Fred Whitton Challenge. Cycling all the road passes in the Lake District in one go in an obvious, beautiful route. Lining up at the start with my confident friend, brimming with fitness and bravado. He said he can do it in under six and a half and me in under seven. I smiled and shook my head. Maybe for him, but for me? No, it won't go.

I had a good ride. Kirkstone, Honister, Newlands, Whinlatter, Cold Fell all came and went. I even felt good riding up the Hardknott. It was only on top of Wrynose when I looked at my watch and realised he was right, it could go. Seven hours and one minute.

Belief. When you lose it you're finished.

It happened eight years ago but I still jump awake at night, feeling the car as it hits me. Turning right onto the trail from a fast road; he was driving too fast and I don't know what was going on in my head. I went over the top of the car and landed on the tarmac. I remember lying there, no pain at first. My first thought? Nothing is more important now than living. Job, house, bike, material shit, none of it matters. I checked I could still wiggle my toes, then lay back and waited for the ambulance. Two days before Christmas, I spent the big day on my bed, concussed and in pain. By New Year I could just about walk. I got on the turbo trainer full of resolution. I wanted to really live.

I need to spend time in beautiful places. Big hills and a big sky keep life in perspective. The mountains have been around for ages. We're not here for very long — you've got to make the most of it. Is that why I do it?

Racing down off Skiddaw, finishing the Bob Graham Round. My friends' loud encouragements ringing in my ears as I beast myself to finish in under 22 hours. The pain of my horribly blistered feet and 65 miles of running over 42 Cumbrian fells is seemingly numbed by this desire. There is a small pointed stone in my shoe, digging right in to a blister on the ball of my left foot, but so what? I'm not going to stop and waste my time by moving it. All I want to do now is finish in under 22 hours. And I do.

And that's it.
Finished.
Is it ever?

INTRODUCTION

The Start Point

'Why do you do eeet?'

The French reporter had a microphone in her hand and a cameraman alongside her. She was standing in the daisies, on the hillside I was climbing with Anna and Chez, in the Chablais Alps above Morzine. My body exhausted and mind weary after five extremely hard days of racing, I thought for a moment before answering.

A few months later, as I sat curled up on my sofa watching the documentary of the race on TV, I had the weird experience of seeing myself trying to answer her simple question.

A simple question with a complex answer, something I am still trying to fathom. Perhaps sometimes the first answer to a question like that is the best.

'Because it's there.'

The famous response of George Mallory when, in 1924, prior to his ill-fated expedition to scale Mount Everest, he was asked why he was attempting to climb the highest mountain in the world. Nowadays these words are a cliché, forming the most frequently used reply (in English at least) when someone is asked why they are attempting something challenging but fundamentally unnecessary.

Although I wasn't attempting to climb Mount Everest, I was at the end of one of the most amazing and physically challenging weeks of my life. In the Haute Savoie department of France, the high Alpine region that lies to the west and south of Mont Blanc, is an area of rugged beauty and an adventurer's paradise. We were coming to the end of the Mountain-X race. A six-day adventure race that encompassed many 'extreme' mountain sports. Competing in teams of three, I was racing with Anna and Chez Frost. Though unrelated they share the same surname, enthusiasm and ability, and I had struggled to keep up with them throughout the week. Anna is a New Zealander who competes at the highest levels in mountain running, representing her country. An experienced expedition guide, mountain biker and all-round adventurer, I had first met Chez while racing against her in the Helvellyn Triathlon. I knew immediately she would be great to race with; her drive, determination and talent is frankly pretty scary.

The Mountain-X was the first time the three of us had raced together. It had worked well, we were a balanced team, supporting each other through the tough times and sharing some emotional moments together. These moments varied from fearfully recovering ourselves, our boat and our paddles to continue racing after we capsized our canoe on rocks in the white water of the Samoëns gorge, to the shared joy of the sunrise as we were high in the mountains on our ascent of the Aiguille des Glaciers.

During each day of the Mountain-X we found ourselves mountaineering, canyoning, mountain biking, rock climbing, white water canoeing or mountain marathon running. Every evening, after the main discipline of the day, there was a shorter, faster mountain running race that really hurt already tired bodies. While these tough days, compounded on each other, were wearing us down, we had been to some amazing places and done some fantastic things: high level mountaineering along a rocky ridge to ascend the Aiguille des Glaciers and to descend across a glacier, mountain biking on stunning singletrack in the beautiful Beaufortain region, via ferrata and rock climbing on a stunning crag high above the Col de Colombière, canyoning in a deep limestone gorge north of Lake Annecy and white water canoeing down some seriously challenging rapids in the Samoëns valley.

The sixth and final day of the race consisted of a nine-hour mountain marathon across the steep ridges and pyramidal peaks of the Chablais Alps. A stage that had started at four in the morning, it was during this last day that the reporter had asked me the question.

The question brought to the surface something that I think I had been mulling over almost subconsciously for some time. I was 31 years old, and had spent much of my free time over the previous ten years rock climbing, biking and running. I started rock climbing and running just before I turned 18. My first experience of climbing was on the polished limestone of the Avon Gorge in my hometown of Bristol during the long summer before I went to university, climbing with some of my friends and teachers from school. Before then I had not spent too much of my time in the outdoors despite particular encouragement from my dad, who loved to spend his time walking in the Brecon Beacons and on Dartmoor.

I had started cycling while at university in Leeds. For the three years of my Maths degree it was my main way of getting around the city, to lectures, pubs and clubs. It wasn't until a couple of years after I finished my degree that I started to cycle longer distances, mainly because it was only then that I could afford a half-decent bike.

As the years progressed, during the decade or so prior to competing in the Mountain-X, I spent more and more of my time challenging myself in physically demanding situations. Invariably surrounded by mountains, the wilder the better, the challenges got harder and harder as my mind and body seemed to grow stronger. Over the years my horizons and beliefs changed. They became broader, and I continually had the urge to seek new challenges to expand and stretch them.

These challenges were sometimes too difficult for my body, too hard for my mind to countenance success, or too much for both, leading to failure. While the feeling of failure was and is always hard to handle, it is in these places that I learned the most about myself, and continue to do so. I hate failing. But if there is not an element of risk or doubt, then where is the challenge? Overcoming fears with belief, fitness and determination is where the drive to succeed is established. In 2008, the year I raced and won the Mountain-X with Anna and Chez, I had earlier completed the Bob Graham Round and, later in the season, won the Three Peaks Cyclo-Cross. In this I achieved two ambitions that five years before I had believed nigh on impossible. I am not a natural athlete; sometimes I look at those who are gifted in this way not with envy but with wonder. What must it be like to be able to be the swiftest, the fleetest of foot? This may sound self-defeatist — I do not mean it to be.

While I am not naturally fast I have a stubborn streak that some-times overrides everything else. This stubbornness is borne of the fact that if I believe something is possible and I think it is worth pursuing, I am driven to achieve it. And that could be anything: completing the Bob Graham, winning the Three Peaks Cyclo-Cross, working towards a PhD, innovation in its many forms, writing a book.

Sometimes this belief in what I can achieve has pushed me close to a physical and mental edge. During the months after the Mountain-X, as I trained for the Three Peaks in the late summer and early autumn, I was also frantically working on finishing my Statistics MSc. Completing the dissertation alongside working full-time and training hard took me to an amazing place mentally and physically. I felt incredibly healthy and alive, despite the fact that I was continually waking at 4 a.m., immediately thinking about my thesis and then working on it for an hour or two before getting on my bike or putting on my running shoes to head out and train before a full day's work. And work. While stimulating, my employment at times drove me crazy. I am still slowly learning the best ways of communicating my ideas to people who think differently to me. I have got it wrong so many times but may now be approaching a point where I get it right and wrong in equal measure. Perhaps in a few years time the scales may tip the other way.

During autumn 2008 I think I reached both a physical and mental peak. At work and during my studies I was exploring new ways of solving mathematical and computational problems while my body was ready to race faster and harder than ever. This was a fascinating time but I knew it could not last; more than that I don't think I wanted it to last. After a peak comes the inevitable drop off in form. In sport your body cannot peak continuously and I don't think in study and innovation the mind can either. I believe pushing your mind too much for too long can lead to mental and emotional damage. Both mind and body need time to bottom-out, rest, recover and recuperate in preparation for the next build-up and peak. Because that is the great thing: if there were no peaks and troughs then everything would stay the same and that would be boring. If there were no troughs then we would never know just how special peaks can be.

After the Mountain-X, and particularly after I had finished my dissertation, I began to actively seek answers to the question. I read more books, something I hadn't done a great deal of since my teenage years. For too long I had ignored the rewarding experiences that reading can bring.

I did not consciously decide where to try and find the answer but, perhaps unsurprisingly as a climber, I started with mountaineering literature. This genre lends itself to so many extreme situations in beautiful places and for years climbing and mountaineering had been my only real passion. Having first climbed on the walls of the Avon Gorge, it was while studying at Leeds University that my hunger for climbing really grew. The gritstone crags of West Yorkshire were a great place to learn. I found climbing and its culture addictive; I lived for the times I spent teetering about on rock faces and cliff edges. When I wasn't in those places I was thinking about them; devouring magazine articles, reading the route guidebooks and talking the talk with my climbing buddies over beers and endless cups of tea. Somehow during this time I managed to acquire a maths degree. While the degree certificate states 'Mathematics BSc', I definitely majored in climbing, and was president of the university mountaineering club in my final year of study. In this club I found lifelong friends.

We experienced intense moments together: fear, achievement, adversity, determination, failure, love and tragedy. We climbed and partied as hard as we could. Living for the moment, we were young and we knew it all.

Climbing is viewed by some people as a sport. For others it is most definitely not a sport; it is a pastime, a way of life.

Some climbers will only ever partake in their sport at a man-made artificial climbing wall. This kind of climbing is almost completely safe, there are bolts to clip the rope into, ensuring any falls are minimal. The serious indoor climber trains for competition and will be lean, fit and honed. Spending time outside climbing is not an effective method of training for these guys.

Other climbers you would never catch anywhere near an indoor climbing wall, or training for that matter. These guys live for the crags of the mountains, sea-cliffs, moorland outcrops and old quarries. As likely to be found enjoying a big greasy pre-climbing breakfast or a few post-climbing pints as they are to be found on the crag, when they are climbing they are doing so for the physical and mental challenge and for the adventure, thrill and beauty of the outdoors.

And the thrill is addictive. Gripping tiny holds, arms screaming and legs wobbling as lactic acid builds up in your muscles, looking to make that crux move on a steep rock face with nothing but the distant ground far below to focus the mind. Nothing else matters but that moment of pure, intense living. The surrounding mountains, sea and sky exemplify the moment. These aged giants are a reminder of mortality; of the end.

Great mountaineering writers like William H Murray, Joe Simpson and Heinrich Harrer describe these extreme moments of living.

'The nearest explanation that I had for why we climbed was that it let us edge along that fine line between life and death, because for a brief moment it changed our perspectives on life. That chance encounter with the dark side made us realise quite how important it was simply to be alive; it made us live.'

This eloquent, honest and perhaps selfish statement of Simpson from his book *The Beckoning Silence* summarises the thrill that so many climbers are addicted to and what many non-climbers do not understand. For me, the title of this book says it all. The intense pull to the edge of death. The extreme moment of danger and challenge that makes you feel so very alive. The book itself is pure Simpson: eloquent, thoughtful and gripping as he recounts his reconciliation of the loss of loved ones, and of his associated need for one last great thrill.

In recent years the British writer and mountaineer Robert MacFarlane has written beautifully and at length, connecting the physical thrill of mountaineering with the spiritual enlightenment offered by time spent in the mountains and wild open spaces. *Mountains of the Mind* is a history of mountaineering in which MacFarlane writes of so much more than the recording of challenging climbs and new lines up mountains and rock faces in far-flung places. The book continually explores the essence of the drive that, through climbing history, has spurred on countless individuals to push their minds and bodies to extremes in their attempts to achieve their lofty ambitions. Early in the book MacFarlane discusses how Western society's collective opinion of mountainous places has changed over the course of the last three hundred years:

'Three centuries ago, risking one's life to climb a mountain would have been considered tantamount to lunacy. The notion barely existed, indeed, that wild landscape might hold any sort of appeal ...

... Over the course of three centuries, therefore, a tremendous revolution of perception occurred in the West concerning mountains. The qualities for which mountains were once reviled — steepness, desolation, perilousness — came to be numbered among their most prized aspects.'

In his second book *The Wild Places* MacFarlane explores the human need for wilderness; where it is, what can be found in it, and why it means so much to us.

'In a land as densely populated as Britain, openness can be hard to find. It is difficult to reach places where the horizon is experienced as a long unbroken line, or where the blue of distance becomes visible. Openness is rare, but its importance is proportionately great. Living constantly among streets and houses induces a sense of enclosure, of short-range sight. The spaces of moors, seas and mountains counteract this. Whenever I return from the moors, I feel a lightness behind my eyes, as though my vision has been opened out by twenty degrees to either side. A region of uninterrupted space is not only a convenient metaphor for freedom and openness, it can sometimes bring these feelings fiercely on.'

I identified so much with this book. It put into words the desire I have to head to the hills, and of how much and how frequently I need them — a fix. The daydreams I have at work of running in the mountains while stuck in the office or at meetings in London exemplify this need. I find it amazing that there are places so contrasting as the claustrophobia and bustle of the London Underground and the release of running in the fells (in my mind as I'm writing it's the Howgills) within hours of each other. For me, the Underground is the unusual place and the fells normality. I want it always to be that way.

Reading books such as these helped to rekindle my love of climbing. In my search for answers it also made me realise it wasn't just me asking the question. In its various guises it is probably the most asked question; those seeking the answer are looking in all sorts of places.

More recently my reading has turned to philosophy and in particular metaphysics. This wasn't really a conscious decision — it just sort of happened. In learning more of this subject, I have realised that there are names for some of the questions and thoughts I have. It also strikes me that there is significant crossover in the questions asked by mountaineers and adventurers and those that philosophers have attempted to answer over the centuries. Should this be surprising? The questions that are stimulated in climbers during or after exposure to very serious and committing situations, to the edge of life and a very real fear of death, are surely the same as those posed and answered by the great metaphysicists. Perhaps the difference is that most climbers come to the questions through practice not via the theory of the philosophers; they are rougher but often more real.

The connection with travelling in and through mountains and philosophical thought is strongly made and discussed at length in Robert M. Pirsig's classic *Zen and the Art of Motorcycle Maintenance*. I think this did the most to help me begin to understand the question I was asking. An astounding and remarkable book, it fascinated me, perhaps more so than any other book I had previously read. In equal measure it scared me. Throughout the book Pirsig is haunted by his former self; the fiercely intelligent, mentally unstable Phaedrus, who was blasted out of his mind by electro-shock treatment some twenty years previous. Mental illness is something that has had a significant impact on my life, particularly so during my adolescent years, learning to cope with the insecurities of having a father who was insane from time to time. Having tried to read the book back then as a teenager, I only actually finished it while in my early thirties, on a solo trip to the Alps road cycling. I am glad both that I returned to it and that I failed to complete it when younger as I don't think I would have appreciated the book as much as I did on my cycling trip, where I found it revelatory.

The days I spent cycling in the mountains, climbing up to high mountain road cols for what seemed like hours on end, combined with evenings spent reading and thinking made my mind race. Pirsig writes of those who choose to spend their time wandering around meta-phorical mountains — those of deep thought — with lucidity.

'The allegory of a physical mountain for the spiritual one that stands between each soul and its goal is an easy and natural one to make. Like those in the valley behind us, most people stand in sight of the spiritual mountains all their lives and never enter them, being content

to listen to others who have been there and thus avoid the hardships. Some travel into the mountains accompanied by experienced guides who know the best and least dangerous routes by which they arrive at their destination. Still others, inexperienced and untrusting, attempt to make their own routes. Few of these are successful, but occasionally some, by sheer will and luck and grace, do make it.'

I felt that the book took me to those places. I had been before. While I do not think I would (or could) spend all of my time there, now that I have been I could not imagine ever wanting to stop going. Connecting with physical mountains is one route to the mountains of the mind. The combination of a healthy mind and body in the mountains is a powerful thing, a heady narcotic. It gives you the belief you need to achieve.

I think this is one reason why I do so miss the hills when I have not seen them for a while. I find solace and strength in these places, they refresh and revitalise me. Sometimes a book, a piece of mathematics, a poem or other art form can serve to soothe my desire for high places. Wandering and wondering can be the same thing. I find challenging thought and deep satisfaction in mathematics, its applications and its beauty. I am so pleased I returned to study a decade after I finished my first degree.

While latterly I have experienced again the thrill of the intellectual challenge of mathematics, the same is true of music and of art. There is such beauty and solace to be found: a life less ordinary.

My mother is a talented musician. In the years after my parents' divorce there was much for her to be stressed and depressed about. Lonely and in a job she hated, she returned to her childhood love for music and began to play the clarinet. From making some quite loud and startling noises to begin with, over the years she progressed, picking up the saxophone and piano along the way. A few years ago, when staying with her, I woke up one morning to hear Chopin being played beautifully, with so much feeling. I felt so proud and lucky that she was my mum.

Not because of the standard she had reached but because of the determination and belief she had to get there. And I know where she was. I arrived there via different routes.

So, why do I do it? I think I will be asking myself that question for a long time yet. I don't think I will ever reach a full answer; maybe sometime soon I'll find I've stopped looking. There is no doubt that some of the reason I do it is to win. To massage my ego, inflate my self-esteem, to make myself materially richer.

I sincerely hope that there are also other reasons, and it is these I wish to explore in this book.

My need for mountains of the mind, body and soul.

PART 1

RISE AND FALL

Wasdale

ONE

FITTING IN

It is always windy in the old quarry on the edge of Ilkley Moor, above the famous Cow and Calf rocks. Today is no different; the heavy greyness of the sky also suggests rain sometime soon. I'd better get myself up this climb a bit faster, so Sarah can have a go at *S-Crack* before the rain starts and we will be forced to beat a retreat to the pub.

I am halfway up *Walewska*, one of a string of classic rock climbs that the quarry contains, and I'm contemplating doing something I have never done before — a handjam.

The rock I am climbing is gritstone. More pedantically, it is Yorkshire gritstone; God's own rock. Gritstone — or grit — is a very rough and hard sandstone which is fantastic to climb on as it offers great friction and gives intricate, challenging problems for climbers to solve as they strive to scale a line. Gritstone crags abound in the north of England, particularly in the Derbyshire Peak District and the moorland above and skirting the edges of pennine towns in North and West Yorkshire. Good climbing can be found on single boulders, in old quarries or on the outcrops untouched by industry but shaped over the millennia by the weather.

These faces can have few holds for hands and feet; perhaps a couple of pebbles to gently pull on. The rounded breaks frequently require force and determination to pass. Climbing on grit demands either pure thuggery or delicate, thoughtful and precise movement; rarely anything between.

Perhaps the most accomplished gritstone climbers are bi-polar; a bizarre combination of thug and ballet dancer.

A handjam is often a useful technique to have up your sleeve when gritstone climbing. Routes frequently offer no handholds apart from narrow rounded breaks. You can wedge your hands in these cracks, and attempt to form a fist. In doing so, your hand effectively forms a camming device inside the break, enabling you to pull on it and progress up the climb.

After a weekend of climbing the backs of our hands would look like we had been fighting; cuts and grazes all over them, suggesting bare-knuckle boxing was our forte, not grappling with rocks out in the wilds of the Yorkshire moors. It wasn't very lady-like but we didn't care. Non-climbing friends would ask what I had been up to at the weekend. One time one of them was aghast when I told her I had spent the weekend sleeping in a cave with my mates, halfway up Stanage Edge. We'd hitched down to the Peak from Leeds for a few days of climbing. We climbed for hours, had a pint or two in the pub (for those who could afford it) and then retreated to the cave for a surprisingly cosy and dry doss before another day of much the same.

Other times we'd hitch to the Lakes for weekends of climbing in the Langdales, drinking in the Old Dungeon Ghyll and then bivvying on the fell behind the pub, or head over to North Wales for adventures in the Llanberis Pass, leaving our bivvy spot by the boulders early to avoid an argument with the 50p lady. All this when we were supposed to be revising for summer exams. No contest.

Many of the friendships I made at the climbing club during my first year at university were ones that would endure. There was an acceptance of people for who they were. Coupled with the routine piss-taking of bullshitters, you had an environment where individuals could be themselves without having to prove anything to anyone or pretend that they were something they were not. Although it generally mattered to the individual and there was a healthy spirit of competition, it didn't really matter how hard you climbed; in fact there were some in the club who hardly climbed at all.

After a first year spent living in university accommodation, in the second year I moved into a shared house with friends from the climbing club. Sarah Church, Ellen Wolfenden ('The Wolf'), Kate Duncan and Kate Fairgrieve. We lived in Woodhouse in Leeds 6, in one of the red brick terrace houses built at the turn of the 20th century. While the postcode district has a high crime rate (once boasting the most burgled street in England), we almost always felt safe; I never had any qualms about going out for a run after dark. Lockable metal gates on the front and back doors were normality, and something we got used to very quickly.

We were never actually burgled which I think was more luck than anything else, given the amount of times someone left the front door unlocked. Maybe it was because they worked out we had nothing worth nicking. We didn't own anything that was technologically state-of-the-art or even with the times; the TV in the lounge was third-hand and on the blink, and that was about it for objects that were approaching being worth stealing. That didn't stop them trying early on, soon after we'd moved in. One night when Kate Duncan was in the house by herself she made a nervous phone call to the police to report that two men were in the process of attempting to break in to the back door's metal gate, just feet away from where she was stood with the phone.

Our house was used as the unofficial club headquarters for that year. It was here that all the club equipment was stored as The Wolf was gear secretary. Behind the sofas in the lounge were a multitude of ropes, ice axes, crampons, helmets and a wide assortment of other climbing hardware that people could borrow. People dropped by to borrow kit, for a brew and frequently after a night's clubbing we had at least two people sleeping in the lounge. One of these regulars was Al Powell, who at the time was teaching over near Halifax and still living in Leeds 6. Having studied at the university prior to entering the world of work, Al was still involved in the climbing club, imparting his knowledge and experience modestly to us wide-eyed freshers. Legendary in the club for his debauched drunken antics as much as his climbing exploits, Al spent his weekends establishing hard new Scottish winter mixed routes, trying to win the Karrimor International Mountain Marathon (KIMM) with his brother Ifor (which they did in 2006), and running and climbing in various mountainous parts of the UK. During school holidays he would be off — to the Alps for shorter trips, and further afield to places such as Greenland and the Himalaya during the longer summer break. Dedicated to new routing and repeating hard established routes, Al was very focused. He would bemoan his climbing partners who forsook these weekends and longer trips away for the sake of spending time with their girlfriends. Once, sat having a cup of tea with the four of us — me, The Wolf, Sarah and Kate Fairgrieve — he complained that one of his usual climbing partners was not going to the Alps that summer but going on safari with his girlfriend:

'Yet another one succumbed to the enemy.'

Raising his eyes from his cup, Al looked around the lounge and realised that he was the only man in the room. He looked slightly sheepish and maybe even a little worried.

'Not you lot obviously. You're alright.'

Now an Alpine guide, Al lives in Otley with his wife Sima and their two young children for most of the year, when he is not away working. Even he succumbed in the end.

The parties held by the climbing club were legendary and it was a well-known rule never to hold the Christmas party at your own house. Each year it was a challenge for the club exec. to find a venue, but eventually some poor fool would volunteer their place. They got a free Christmas dinner but also a whole heap of mess to clear up. Always fancy-dress, outlandish costumes abounded; one time the theme was 'the sea' and Dave, a fiercely intelligent guy doing a PhD in Mechanical Engineering, came dressed as a giant lobster. He must have spent ages on his costume: his huge claws were combined works of art and science, perfectly to scale with working hinges. Keeping with the marine theme, Al orchestrated a surfing competition: down the stairs on an ironing board. Geordie Nick won.

Sarah's boyfriend Dom was a man of many layers. When I joined the club as a fresher he was president and everyone knew and liked him. He was funny, gregarious and could be extremely lazy, but also so very focused and hard working when he chose to be, and generally his focus was on climbing. He could recite climbing guidebooks to the letter, so voraciously did he read them, planning his next adventures. Dom had a scar that spanned the length of his body, starting near his shoulder and ending at his ankle. It was acquired when he was struck by lightning while climbing in the Alps. Very well read and intelligent, he was a Catholic who had spent some time training to be a priest. A student of Philosophy and Russian (until he got thrown off the course for attending no lectures and doing no work), he was extremely good on the trumpet. One night we went to watch him playing at the Hyde Park Club, in a soul-funk band whose lead-singer was another climber, a guy called Arne.

One of my lasting images of Arne is of him skiing down the Goat Track Gully on Coire an t-Sneachda in the Cairngorms. We were climbing a route on a buttress adjacent to the gully, and watched him as he telemark-turned in the tight confines of this snow-filled gap. I had never seen anyone ski down as narrow a place before; Arne did it with style and grace and with a massive smile on his face. Whenever I saw him and whatever he was doing, he always looked like he was enjoying himself. I knew him for a year, and in that year I saw him skiing, climbing, singing, studying, dancing, smiling: living. He and Dom were peas in a pod; so varied in their pursuits, and so focused, but doing it for the plain reason that it made them feel alive. It was no surprise that the two of them got on so well.

Dom lived with Sarah in our house. That year she started her PhD and Dom, no longer at the university, took temporary work in between spells spent entirely climbing. In the autumn he got a job at the Leeds Wall — the relatively new climbing wall that had opened on the Gelderd Road. This was better for him and more satisfying than the factory work, although typically for Dom, he lost this job when he chose to go climbing on Ben Nevis in Scotland rather than work. Winter climbing conditions that weekend were superb; among other ascents, he and Sarah climbed *Smith's Route*. This was one of his longstanding ambitions, no doubt due to its physical challenge, but for Dom it would have also been important for its aesthetics, history and association with the legendary Robin Smith. I don't think he regretted his choice.

In the summer of 1997, Sarah headed to Iceland to spend eight weeks on a glacier for her fieldwork. The Wolf went to the Alps to do the fieldwork that would form the basis for her Geology degree dissertation. Various climbing trips to the Alps were planned; I was heading out with Anna, a philosophy lecturer from the university. While there, we would meet up with the other guys who, when not on the hill, would be ensconced on the cheapest campsite in Chamonix. These included Dom and Arne, who planned to spend a month based in the valley, climbing together.

I began the three-month university summer holiday with four weeks working at a National Trust centre in Pembrokeshire, climbing on the limestone sea cliffs at weekends and in the evenings. This was followed by a week-long trip to the Scottish island of Arran with Aidan. We had been together since the previous Christmas; it was our first holiday. We spent it climbing and running up, around and over the amazing hills and crags found on Goat Fell and the stunning Glen Rosa horseshoe.

We returned to Leeds to the news that Dom and Arne were missing in the Alps. They had been gone for four days, and no one wanted to believe what this meant. In Alpine mountaineering, climbers can be a day or so late returning to the valley after completing a route but, any more than that, and people start to seriously worry about their well-being. Five days after first hearing that Dom and Arne had not returned to their campsite, four of Dom's closest friends from the climbing club headed out to Chamonix with his brother, James, to see if they could try and find them.

It was on the radio that I first heard that their bodies had been found; such a common way to first hear news but this time the normal, impersonal acknowledgement of such events was not there. They were spotted on a glacier, amongst avalanche debris, by a helicopter that was in the process of rescuing some other climbers. Still roped together, evidently they had both been swept down in the avalanche they probably themselves triggered when climbing unstable wet snow in the heat of the day. Despite knowing that this was all too likely to have happened given the length of time they had been missing, it was unbelievable, just not real.

Sarah loved him so much and she had to be told. I contacted her dad and the university geography department, and soon she was travelling back to the UK with her PhD supervisor. When she got back, her dad picked her up from the airport and took her to his house down south. A day later we got a quiet phone call; she wanted to be up in Leeds, in her house, with us. As close as she could get to Dom.

Her grief was raw, her eyes inconsolable with hollow pain. We tried our best to take care of her; I worried so much about upsetting her further, saying something that triggered memories that were so painful in those early days. In time, over weeks and then months, I started to feel resentful of this worry; it was almost a burden. Looking back today, counting Sarah as one of my closest friends, I understand better. There was nothing that I could have said or done that would have made her feel worse. Soothing grief takes time; Sarah was beginning her journey with us, and taking whatever comfort from that she could. Nothing we said to her would make much of a difference to her pain; having us around was the important thing.

More people had come back to Leeds – The Wolf temporarily back from her fieldwork, both Kates and other friends. Evenings were spent at our house, ordering takeaways, getting pissed and talking. Being together made a difference to us all.

Both funerals took place on beautiful summer days, a few days apart. Arne's family lived on a farm in the rolling Dorset hills. His father requested Arne's climbing friends carry him from the house and through their village on the way to the funeral service; his family and friends from home carried him to his grave. The village church was filled to bursting with people from all sorts of lives, dressed in all sorts of ways. All were made so welcome by Arne's family. Afterwards, in the evening and into the next morning we partied for him. His band played, we danced and danced.

Then to Shropshire, where Dom's family lived in Telford. During the service we heard how varied his life had been, and just what a gap his passing had left for so many people. Dom had an impact on the people he met and spoke with, sharing his thoughts, his passions and his observations on life, and listening to those of others. I could understand why he began training as a priest, and also why he left this training. I sometimes wonder where Dom would be today; perhaps somewhere entirely different, perhaps somewhere writing a book about the varied and fascinating adventures he had experienced as he made his own path.

Their funerals were very different. But during both, two butterflies flew together above the altar, upwards into the sunlit spire. Two spirits free? 'They are not free, they are dead,' I remember thinking bitterly. I had no time for signs, spiritual or otherwise; I didn't care for placations. Dom and Arne were not with us anymore; two friends who loved living — possibly too much to stay with us for as long as all of us wanted and some of us needed — were gone.

For the rest of the summer and autumn it seemed that whenever I went climbing I saw butterflies: a windy day at Rylstone, during rain at Holyhead Mountain, Millstone Edge, the Cromlech and in the

Lake District's Duddon Valley. They were there, fluttering and basking in the sun. My classicist mind still tells me it must have been a good year for them; that there was some scientific explanation, even though the last time that year I saw them was during a mild mid-December day, while climbing at Birchen Edge in the Peak District. Butterflies in December?

Climbers — in particular mountaineers — who spend many years pushing themselves in high places become familiar with losing friends. It is generally not spoken about, and it almost feels wrong to write about it here, but it happens, and sadly all too frequently. The acceptance that the lifestyle people choose to lead, the challenges they pursue and risks they choose to take in this pursuit is difficult for some; loved ones left behind and bereft are hard to console. I will never forget the expressions of Dom and Arne's mothers at each of their funerals. The same look of loss, so deep and intense, that it was hard to perceive, let alone feel in a position to offer comfort. It felt like nothing would be sufficient to ease each mother's grief; robbed of her treasure, her young man — a man only at the beginning of fulfilling himself with what his individual vitality suggested was within his grasp.

Dom's family wanted his ashes scattered somewhere he had loved. The Llanberis Pass in Snowdonia, on the hillside between the Cromlech and Dinas Mot, was the natural choice. In May, earlier that year, Dom and Sarah had returned to Leeds buzzing after a weekend of climbing achievement, the highlights of which were two classics on the Cromlech: *Cemetery Gates* for Sarah and *Left Wall* for Dom. He loved North Wales. So, in the late summer, we all met in Pete's Eats and drove up the Pass. It was a quiet day, coincident with the funeral of Princess Diana, and it seemed many other people had stayed at home.

In the days after we learned that Dom and Arne had died, it seemed unkind, hurtful even, to go climbing. It felt like to do so was dismissive of what had happened, and how it had changed my perceptions of life and death. When I got knocked off my mountain bike by a car some three years later, I remember being angered by a phone call with my aunt. She had said that the car accident was a reminder of my own mortality; that I was not impermeable to harm. I was pissed off by that because I knew it already, and at the time was so angry with myself for not caring enough about that fact that I had put myself at so much risk. I should have controlled things better.

After a few covert trips bouldering to Caley Crags near Otley, we started heading off on trips again. Our climbing lives went on; Dom and Arne would have expected nothing less, indeed when I started tying into the rope and climbing routes again, I felt Dom's voice in my head, teasing me about my discomforts and encouraging me to forget them and go for it.

A few days after we had scattered Dom's ashes in the Pass, a group of us were beginning the walk-in to Cyrn Las, a high-mountain crag on the side of Snowdon. In my sights was *Main Wall*, the classic easy climb of the face, Hard Severe in grade, renowned for its exposure and Alpine-like feel. As we started walking we passed a pair of climbers sat by the roadside, one of them was Angela Soper. At the time I was president of the university climbing club, and one of my aims for the coming year was to encourage a few more experienced climbers with stories to tell to come to the Packhorse pub on a Wednesday night and give a talk to us all. Angela would fit the bill perfectly; in retirement she was still pushing the grade, and had been around the world with her climbing exploits. We would see her down the Leeds Wall, cranking it out on the bouldering wall or the steepest sections of the main lead wall.

I pushed my shyness aside, walked up to the pair of them and introduced myself. Angela was more than happy to come and give a talk to the club. Furthermore, she and her climbing partner were also heading up to Cyrn Las. Angela had in her sights *Lubyanka*, another noted climb of the crag, this time the hard classic at E2 6a. This route shares belay stances with *Main Wall*, and for much of the time I was climbing Angela was also leading her route. As I led the hardest pitch of my route, I started to get unnerved by the exposure on the mountain crag, and began to have fairly vocal jibber. Unfazed and seemingly undistracted by the noise I was making, from the crux of her route, Angela spoke a few words of encouragement to me. She was so calm and graceful, and climbed with an elegance that had its roots in the strength, determination and belief she had developed from her many years of hard climbing. I found her a real inspiration.

And that's one of the great things about climbing; the inspirational people you meet from all walks of life. So bound by a love for what they do and how they do it that there is an immediate common understanding and dialogue; the ice gets broken very quickly. In a lot of ways the university club was a microcosm of this; a real mix of students, ex-students, dropouts (who had realised that there are better things to do than studying), lecturers and more. We weren't bound by an academic subject or even a sport as such. We were connected by a pastime, a way of life that, while embodied in the activity of climbing mountains and rocks, was a lot more besides. It was my first real experience of being among people with the same values, and for being accepted for who I am.

Mont Blanc du Tacul summit with Sarah Fuller, August 1996. *Photo: Ellen Wolfenden*

TWO

MOUNTAIN MARATHON 1

'Do not go where the path may lead,
go instead where there is no path and leave a trail.'
RALPH WALDO EMERSON

The clag was settled firmly on the hilltops, forming an almost impen-etrable layer of gloom. The rain was steady and incessant; the feeling of dread inside me was worsening. Ellen — The Wolf — was stood beside me; we were in a queue of other pairs on the side of the hill, next to a muddy track that led nowhere. It was 1996, the last Saturday in October. We were in the Galloway Hills, in south-west Scotland, waiting to each be handed a map and start our first mountain marathon.

Rather different from a road running marathon, where the distance is always 26.2 miles and the terrain flat asphalt, a mountain marathon is considerably more varied. Held over two days, these events are essentially long fell races, with the added elements of challenging ori-enteering and an overnight wild-camp. Racers compete in teams of two and between them have to carry all the camping equipment, food and clothes required to ensure that they are adequately fed, sheltered, and warm throughout the weekend. On the start line each competitor receives a map which has been marked with a series of checkpoints. The map will cover a significant area of mountainous terrain, typically with few and limited paths, and the checkpoints will be located on features on the map. These need to be navigated to and visited, in order, throughout the first day of the race, finishing the day at the overnight camp, which invariably will be exposed and remote. Here competitors rest up, try to stay warm, eat and sleep in preparation for the next day, where, in a repeat of the first, competitors must locate a series of different checkpoints as they travel from the camp to the race finish.

Within the event itself there are different categories or courses. These vary in distance, ascent and navigational difficulty and there are normally at least four of them — Elite, A, B and C. While course C will be the easiest of the event, it is no walkover; over the weekend, racers on this course can expect to cover 50 kilometres and ascend 2000 metres as a minimum. As the majority of this distance will be covered on open moorland, without paths to both enable faster running and act as a guide, it will be a very tough 50 kilometres, incomparable with the equivalent road running distance on smooth and level ground.

Both the distance and the ascent will vary for each team within the same category. The map handed out at the start will have the checkpoints marked on, but the decision of how to get to each of these checkpoints is left to the competitors. This is where orienteering skills and hill-going experience are tried and tested.

The planners of these races are canny. They will strive to ensure that there are at least two choices to be made regarding the best and fastest way between checkpoints, and it will not be immediately clear which is the fastest. A classic choice is to place two checkpoints on either side of a steep valley; competitors must choose between traversing the valley rim or descending to the valley floor and then climbing out. The latter will be more direct, with less distance to cover but more climbing, and could well take more time than the flatter but longer choice of following the contour. Strategically, it could be better for runners to choose the traverse, even if it may take a little longer, as it will leave the legs less tired towards the end of the day, enabling a faster pace and clearer head over the last few miles. It is also important to consider the terrain when it comes to route choice.

Valley floors can often be tussocky and boggy — slower going than the grassy ridge above. Boggy ground and tussocks not only slow you down they are also draining so it is important to avoid these where possible.

Added to all of these route choice challenges is the difficulty posed by navigation. Often hills are clad in a layer of cloud or mist. It may be windy and raining — perhaps even snowing. All these elements reduce visibility and this is where the map becomes even more important, and so too a compass. There is something incredibly satisfying about using these as a guide when you cannot see where you are going. Likewise, literally losing your bearings can be a very frustrating, confusing and at times even a dangerous situation. When it happens, learning how to place yourself, retracing steps and using every piece of available information around you — the direction of north, the slope of the hillside, any feature such as a stream or wall — is imperative. Initially it can be hard to place complete trust in a map and compass — their effective use is based entirely on the individual having the skills and knowledge of how to use them. These skills and knowledge take time and a commitment to acquire, and they are things that can always be improved, whatever your level of competence. I think it is amazing that a two dimensional image and an object whose only consistency is that it points north can be used in this way. And their strength is in their combination; while one is useful without the other, their utility is increased more than two-fold when together.

In the UK fell running, orienteering and hill walking circles, the Original Mountain Marathon, or OMM, is renowned. Held annually over the last weekend in October in a remote and hilly area, the race gets its fair share of challenging weather conditions. The race organisers have always been open about the fact that the event is intended not only to test competitors' abilities to move fast and accurately in the hills, but also to handle and cope with the inclement weather that happens fairly frequently at this time of year. As such, the organisers state explicitly that competitors should be competent on the hill, carry the equipment required to maintain their safety, and expect to experience some levels of discomfort throughout the weekend. These factors do not detract from the popularity of the race. The first event was held in 1968 in the Northern Pennines. Over the years, the race developed a reputation as one that fully tested an individual's hill-going skills and experience. Events such as the one held in Galloway in 1976 when there were blizzards, and another held in the Howgill Fells in 1998 when there were fierce storms, have made it infamous. This infamy stokes its popularity and demand for entries is such that it is normally over-subscribed and the three thousand or so places are filled by lottery.

In 2008 the event gained wider notoriety as it made the news head-lines of the BBC, who reported that over one thousand runners were missing on the fells of Borrowdale in the Lake District — an area at the time receiving some of the worst autumn storms and subsequent flooding in years. The underlying implication of the report was that these runners were lost and in peril; an impending mass tragedy on the fell side. In all actuality, while there were over one thousand run-ners out on the fell, they were not missing (they knew where they were as they each had a map), they were not in any immediate peril (the rules of the OMM state that runners must carry 36 hours worth of food and the tent, sleeping bag and other equipment required to camp out for the night) and, while they were probably experiencing some discomfort, most were relishing their time away from the controlled and controlling aspects of today's society that led to such an over reaction by the media.

As the weekend unfurled (the organisers made the decision on the Saturday afternoon to cancel the race and neutralised it from then on), I watched the news emerge on the internet from my sofa. While I had entered the race that year, my teammate Janet had not recovered from injury in time for us to race together, and that weekend was also the very last one before the very last deadline for the completion of my MSc dissertation. As I still had to fully write-up my thesis and I had struggled to find a new teammate, I stayed home.

It was a funny weekend for me; so intensely working on my write-up and conscious of the ticking clock, but also very frustrated that I was missing out on the race and all that it entails. Aidan was racing with a friend so I was home alone, jealous of him and all my other friends out on the fells, but my the deadline was looming and I did not want to delay my MSc for another year. I watched the news with disbelief as it proclaimed a large-scale tragedy was only hours away. As it happened, the 3000 or so competitors suffered less minor and major injuries than is to be expected of this kind of race annually. There were two broken legs and a number of other incidents where runners required assistance getting off the fell.

In the days and weeks after the event, the media tried to explain just why thousands of people (normal people, rather like themselves really) chose to spend a weekend of misery in a flooded and storm-ridden Lake District. Listening to the radio and reading the paper, I found it really interesting (and also at times rather frustrating) to read of and to hear other peoples' opinions: opinions of those who could not understand the attraction, the urge to spend time in the hills, enjoying the environment, and coping with what it throws up. Our litigation culture made these people point the finger at the race organisers for knowingly sending thousands of runners to their doom. The organisers pointed out that competitors were obliged to state their levels of competency in the hills by providing details of their previous experience, moreover they carried the appropriate equipment and — perhaps most importantly — that each individual competitor had chosen to start, well aware of the weather forecast and the requirements on themselves, their equipment and their experience that this weather brought with it. This was the key difference between the attitude of the race organisers and that of the media majority; the former assumed the experience and knowledge of those competing, the latter did not. Perhaps those decrying the irresponsibility of both the organisers and competitors were ascribing their own low levels of competence onto people they neither knew or understood. In doing so they missed the point.

All this can be construed as the harsh and downright miserable side of spending a weekend in the hills, being self-sufficient as you endeavour to locate checkpoints, handle the challenges of being wet, cold and hungry and finishing the race. It all sounds rather masochistic; where is the fun in it? The escapism is answer in itself; in his great book about the obsessions and elation of fell-running, *Feet in the Clouds*, Richard Askwith writes of his experiences of the Lowe Alpine Mountain Marathon (LAMM), a classic race that takes place in the Scottish Highlands every June. He describes the fulfilment that can be found spending a weekend away from the normality and contradictions of everyday life:

'We are richer now, but also more overworked, more deeply in thrall to the addictions of getting and spending. We have more possessions and they tyrannise us … We have more, and we have less. In such a world, freedom is both more precious and more elusive than ever. And one of the surefire ways of liberating ourselves from the tyranny of consumer society is to put ourselves beyond its reach.'

He also writes of just how easy it is, immediately after the event, to forget what you have just experienced, and fall back into routine:

'After leaving the airport — still less than four hours after the finish — I find myself stuck in a motorway tailback on the final stretch to Northamptonshire. I drum my dashboard in frustration and worry that my rickety old Renault may be about to overheat. Damn. Maybe it's time to cut my losses and get something slightly newer — except that I haven't any money, and, even if I had, I'd need it for repairs to the house … Then I pause for a moment and think. How quickly I have become re-entangled.'

Mountain marathons give us a means to get away from the routine. Of course, the beauty of the remote places and terrain in which they take place is also an attraction. I have so many lasting memories of amazing vistas; cloud suddenly clearing to reveal a rugged, rock crested ridge line, mysteriously disappearing into a lower layer of mist; the wonderful contrasting colours of brown bracken against the green of a grassy hillside, glowing in low autumnal light. So many memories, whose simple recollection makes my mind race.

One of the reasons television programmes about nature, walking and wild places are so popular is that they give us the opportunity to imagine being in a different place to our armchairs, relaxing after what was possibly a stressful, frustrating or boring day at work; imagining being in these different places, with the thrills that they can bring. It's safe escapism, of the mind and not the body, in the comfort of our own homes. In reality, actually being in these other places can often be challenging in a different way. Quite apart from the fact that natural and wild environments can be harsh places to be, our familiarity with society and being with and around other people leads us to feel at times that the urge to spend time away from the trappings of society is wrong; we must all conform to meet the behavioural expectations of our peers. You could say that mountain marathons are themselves contrived; they are a controlled way to get away for a weekend before returning to normality, as Askwith describes above.

Back in 1995 — my first year at university — the OMM was called the Karrimor International Mountain Marathon (KIMM). The Wolf and I had heard about the race from my uncle, and from friends in the climbing club at university, who at the end of October had returned, full of pride and bravado, from completing the B class course in the Brecon Beacons. Having listened to our friends' boasts, our envy at their weekend of adventure, and our hankering for something similar more than encouraged us to enter the race the year after.

In the months preceding the event we had climbed in loads of places including the Verdon Gorge, the sea cliffs of Pembrokeshire, Fontainebleau and the Chamonix Aiguilles, and we had gone for a few runs on the well-trodden paths on Ilkley Moor. We were confident that we were more than ready to tackle the C course.

And so, there we were, on a wet hillside in Galloway, wondering what the hell was going on. Everything was new to me.

The Wolf said that she could read a map — handy, as I could not. And a compass? I had never owned or even used one. We could look after ourselves on the hill; our time climbing in the Alps and in Scotland in the winter helped us to gain the experience to be able to take care of ourselves but, for me at least, navigation was novel.

We were each handed a map and our race began.

To begin with, we had to mark on our maps the checkpoints we had to visit in order to complete the day's course. I found six-figure grid references reasonably familiar; a combination of vague recollections from GCSE geography and the fact that it was all very graph-related made marking the map up fairly straightforward — I was doing a maths degree after all. Unfortunately, this was where my knowledge began and ended. The map's swirls and lines meant nothing to me. I resolved to follow The Wolf.

The Wolf's confidence belied her experience of using a map and compass in anger. She could read a map but she wasn't as good at it as she thought. In situations like these, over confidence can be a bad thing. Given my level of experience at the time it was not for me to criticise. I followed, we got lost, we found ourselves, we got lost again, we got hungry, I force-fed The Wolf malt loaf and insisted she put some more clothes on. We shouted at each other, stumbled over tussocks, got lost, fell into small streams, struggled to cross fierce streams in spate (which became more numerous as the day went on), found ourselves on the summit of The Merrick (the largest of the Galloway Hills) and — finally — we reached the overnight camp.

It had been a truly great day.

We erected The Wolf's heavy but stable tent, which we'd been carrying around all day, and got into it and our sleeping bags. The weather had been very wet and windy and stayed like that through the evening and into the night. Many competitors had retired from the race and gone home. This often happens with the OMM — when the weather is particularly poor it is not uncommon for at least a third of the field to accept their limits and retire. This can be particularly so for competitors on the harder and longer courses such as the A and Elite — the distances and difficulties are such that bad weather can itself decide for many teams between success and failure.

There were around a thousand people on the boggy field that formed our campground for the night. Everyone was doing the same sorts of things, cooking, eating, chatting about their day, their route choices and the weather. After a dinner of quick-cook noodles, cake and custard, energy drink and jelly babies, we fell asleep.

During the night it got windier and wetter. From the comfort of our tent and sleeping bags, the following day of more running, this time on tired legs and blistered feet, felt entirely unattractive and something that I downright did not want to happen. At around 2 a.m., The Wolf's words echoed my thoughts.

'Heather, I don't want to do it today.'

Morning arrived later than the day before as the clocks had gone back an hour. At around 6 a.m. the campsite started to stir; people began brewing tea and eating muesli, porridge and other such high carb foods. The occasional whiff of bacon made me very jealous of those who had carried it in to the campsite with them. While struggling to chew my muesli, I considered how painful running on my blistered feet was going to be. I wasn't in a good frame of mind to begin the second day and, given her furrowed brow and shared struggle to eat breakfast, neither was The Wolf.

But start we did; straight across a river in spate that the organisers had put a rope across for fear of competitors getting washed away, and then immediately up a steep hill. We were generally heading in the same direction as many other teams moving at a similar pace and figured we were probably all on the same category — the C course. Occasionally, whippet-like fast moving teams would run past us. Their rucksacks were much smaller than our own and they had a determined, knowing look in their eye. We figured they were doing the A or Elite courses. These categories were far harder than ours, more ascent, a further distance to cover, trickier route choice and tougher navigation; all in a far, far tougher proposition and something I could never envisage doing. Moreover, I did not see any women racing these courses. Perhaps understandably so, given that the toughness of the Elite course in particular is renowned to test the hardest of men; each day covering the distance of a full marathon with upwards of 2000 metres of ascent. These were categories for people like Al Powell, who raced the Elite course annually with his brother Ifor.

After our legs had warmed into the climbing of steep hills and traversing the rough, tussock-ridden terrain of Galloway, we found the second day easier than the first. Not only was there slightly less distance to cover, the weather had improved and there were lots of people to follow. In mountain marathons, particularly those the size of the OMM, 'snakes' form during the second day as lots of racers in shorter categories with less route choice all go the same way, thereby forming a trod and then a path: the 'snake'. For much of the day we were in one of these snakes and were frankly pretty happy with it; there was less need to read the map and we clearly had fresher legs than some others. We regained some enthusiasm and even started overtaking a few people.

The last descent off the hill above the finish line was painful on the body but very satisfying. During the weekend we had learned so much, and had gone from not really knowing what was going on to under-standing what it was we needed to do to further develop in order to be more competent and able in environments such as the stormy Gal-loway Hills. I don't think that our confidence in being able to finish the event was misplaced but I do think that we were not 'more than ready'.

We were just about ready, and completing the C course in unusually challenging weather conditions had shown this to be the case.

There was no way we would have finished without The Wolf's ability to read the map. At the time, my map reading skills were non-existent so I really should not have bemoaned her own level of ability. The weekend had been testing for both of us. We had argued and shouted at each other, using strong words from time to time. I had only known Ellen for just over a year but already counted her as one of my closest friends. We'd had a rather desperate time together on a rock-climbing route on the Aiguille de l'M in the Chamonix valley over the summer, which had strengthened our friendship as well as made us aware that we could both handle the extremes of screaming at each other one minute and then laughing together the next.

We ran down a very muddy path through a forest to reach a field on the valley bottom and the finish. Crossing the line we were all smiles and hugged each other warmly. Both of us had a real sense of achievement at succeeding in something so new and so testing. We were way down the field in the order of finishers of the C course but we didn't even think of that; it did not matter. What mattered was that we had finished something that both of us, at times over the weekend, had felt was too hard, too much of a challenge.

Those Elite guys that ran past us as we climbed the first hill seemed like gods. I simply could not fathom the levels of skill and fitness they had developed to be able to move with such confidence and speed.

As we stood in a long queue, waiting to be handed the plate of hot steaming chilli, cup of tea and cake every finisher receives, I resolved to do the OMM again, and to spend time working on the skills that were required in such events. I did not have any lofty ambitions — not beyond the B class at least — I just wanted to come back and perhaps next time help decide route choice, which direction to head in and to make less mistakes. I was 19 and Ellen had just turned 20 — we had plenty of time to learn.

I think even then I knew where I wanted to get to. Those Elite guys; doing something that looks so easy, carrying it out with a style and grace that belies the years of practice, the failures, the learning, more failures — honing the skills required for it to appear effortless. I aspired to be more like them. I was already hooked on mountain marathons; sucked in by the beauty of traversing mountains, the need to interpret the shape of the terrain from both the ground and the map and to be able to move across it with confidence.

During my short time in the mountains walking, climbing and running, I had experienced the freedom and liberation found in being at one with a wild, and at times hostile, place — and of coping with the mental and physical challenges implicit within this hostility. All this is a means of escape from the ordinary — the mundane, the futile, the boring. Which brings me back to those who questioned the rights of those competing in the OMM in 2008 to do just that. I make my own informed choice to spend time running in the hills.

Why should any individual need to justify this to anyone else?

THREE

SEA CLIFFS

A Dream of White Horses. Poetic words that instil a sense of excitement and fear in the mind of any aspirant sea-cliff climber.

On the north-west coast of the island of Anglesey, just off the north-west coast of Wales, are a series of steep sea cliffs. Popular with walkers, bird-watchers and other nature enthusiasts, the clifftops and edges are laden with flora and fauna, sand lizards and puffin burrows. The rare chough can also often be seen, its red beak and shank contrasting with jet-black plumage, swooping around on thermals, giving the trademark call.

These same sea cliffs have another side, an underside. In the rock climbing world these cliffs are infamous.

This darker side is a reflection of the ragged bunches of crag rats — climbers — that appeared in the 1960s to explore and to seek out new, daring and often outrageous lines up the sheer cliff faces. The numbers of these climbers increased through the 1970s and 1980s. They came from the mountains and slate mines of Snowdonia, seeking a new arena on which to get their fix. That arena was the steep and intimidating playground that is Craig Gogarth.

A mythical-sounding place (perhaps the lair of some Middle Earth evil being), Gogarth is home to some of the finest sea cliff climbing in the UK. A place to go for adventure climbing and at Gogarth the new routing protagonists have always been true adventure climbers.

Johnny Dawes, Paul Pritchard, John Redhead and other renowned anarchistic and naturally-gifted climbers. Artists rather than athletes — while in possession of prodigious strength, it was often more subtle skills that enabled these guys to climb their audacious new routes. Anyone who has seen the film *Stone Monkey*, in which Dawes plays a starring role, will have been wowed by the way he climbs *The Quarryman*, his legendary route in the Llanberis slate mines. The line of the route is formed by a steep dierdre — a corner — with practically no hand or footholds and nowhere in which to place protection. Dawes' style is unique as he ascends. He is at one with the cliff face, working with it, not attempting to fight it with brute force but using an elegance more akin to a talented dancer. A real artist.

Such subtle skills, combined with an appreciation for the aesthetics of a new line and possibly a hint of madness, enabled these climbers to establish routes of unremitting difficulty on the cliffs of Gogarth and the quarries and mountain crags of Snowdonia. For a while North Wales was the hotbed of new-routing activity in the UK. These activists forsook everything for their love of climbing. They were skint, hungry, cold and unhealthy. Sometimes out of choice and sometimes out of necessity.

In his book *Deep Play* Paul Pritchard discusses how, in the 1980s, Thatcher's Britain did more to enable these crag rats than was perhaps intended:

'When it came to leave school most of my friends either signed on as unemployed or went on government job creation schemes. The ones that signed on had free time to develop sometimes obscure skills that seemed at first to have no use to the community. Later this would be seen not to be the case as, throughout the country, champion runners and cyclists and famous painters and writers emerged.'

The great changes that the then-government pummelled through the UK economy saw industries end; whole towns massively impacted by the closure of their main employer. The job for life was becoming a thing of the past. Those part-way through their working lives did not know which way to turn. And what of the young, just beginning on this journey? The opportunities for success were there, but so too were the opportunities for failure. The artistry and alternative communities that developed and grew during this time of high unemployment and the dole were a by-product of what has since been called a lost generation.

'But for us youngsters, this was now the land of opportunity, the government told us anything could be ours. We were free to gamble, but if we failed, we would be at the bottom of the heap.'

Pritchard and his vagabond climbing friends at times chose and at times were pushed into the alternative. The rock became their workplace. While there was not much of Thatcher's material richness, the rewards that could be found in this lifestyle were more than enough to justify the means.

'Out of the ashes of this social, economic and moral turmoil the full-time climber rose like some scruffy, bedraggled phoenix to push the boundaries of what was possible on our crags, quarries and sea cliffs.'

Those ecstatic moments of success, of extending the possible, had huge satisfaction. Perhaps the manner in which these moments had been achieved — they were at least in part borne out of pure rebellion to the behaviours the Establishment were working to instil in society — added to this satisfaction.

In his 2002 biography of the great Scottish mountaineer Dougal Haston *The Philosophy of Risk*, Jeff Connor uses extracts from Haston's diaries to explore the man and his drive. In one section Haston explores his need to continually push himself:

'I still feel the urge to fight with the forces of unknown walls.
It has become a necessary part of life for me ...

... These tests are not stepping stones to one big test. They exist as separate wholes, the tackling of which is one complete function in my term of existence. The results of the continuous on self and general action is being observed carefully, I am becoming more complete.

... Often certain of the attitudes are called selfishness. The latter is a sin in the eye of the masses. Why? They are too conditioned to mass thinking.

... One has freedom at birth. Why should one submerge or lose this freedom in attempting to help others who also has this, but lost it? The masses are not free, as they become bound by the morass of cant which rules society. Most accept a life sentence in the imprisonment of general rulings. The freedom we are born with is the freedom to live as freely as possible within certain laws. This is the freedom I pursue.'

Haston is discussing the relationship between libertarianism and the need to push oneself further and further. If you can slip some of the trusses by which society attempts to bind us, with that freedom comes a need to explore your self, and to test it.

Pritchard's additions to Gogarth were awe-inspiring and fearsome lines. His book describes new-routing on the Red Wall; such new lines as *The Enchanted Broccoli Garden* and *Super Calabrese*. Gogarth has a reputation for steep and intimidating climbing, with lots of loose rock and little or no protection. Pritchard's achievements on its walls — routes at the cutting edge of difficulty and aestheticism — were therefore significant. As with Dawes' *Quarryman*, they required far more than pure physical strength.

It was a muggy Saturday in August. We had headed to Gogarth from the mountain crags of Nant Peris on the side of Snowdon to avoid the crowds in the Pass, and to seek out a refreshing sea breeze to take the sting out of the heat of the afternoon while climbing.

I was climbing with Nirvana, a friend from Leeds University Mountaineering club. I didn't know Nirvana very well but I liked her and I liked to climb with her. She was a quiet and thoughtful person, who seemed to be in possession of a large amount of determination. She was also in possession of her boyfriend's large, fast red car for the weekend and on Friday night we had made record time from the back-to-backs of Leeds 6 to the mountains of North Wales.

Nirvana and I had started the day on *The Ramp*: a two-pitch route on Gogarth's main cliff. Graded Hard Very Severe (HVS), we were pretty comfortable climbing at that level. We found it straightforward and enjoyable; both leading a pitch and finding no undue pressure from the technical climbing or our own preparedness.

'Leading' means climbing first, heading up the rock face tied into the rope, but with it always below you. 'Seconding' is the opposite to leading, and this is when the second climber follows their partner up a pitch after they have led it.

The leader places protection — essentially metal wedges and camming devices — in the cracks and seams of the rock as they climb. The rope is attached to the protection by a karabiner or quickdraw which means that if the leader falls they should not fall the entire length of the distance they have climbed — the last piece of protection they have placed should hold them and therefore shorten the distance of the fall. I say 'should' because the protection is temporary, and will be removed by the second as they climb up the rock face, following after the leader has finished their pitch. The leader requires a level of skill and experience, both to find cracks and fissures into which to place protection and to ensure that, in the event of a fall, this protection will not rip out of the crack; it will stay wedged into the rock and hold the falling climber.

Climbing higher above the last placed piece of protection risks a larger fall. This is where the mind games come in. The line you are climbing may be well within your physical limits but, if your head isn't together, that climb won't go today. You back off, frustrated, angry perhaps. Your climbing partner leads through; their head is in a better place. You become the second, and with it come feelings of failure, as climbers know it is only the lead that really counts.

Counter to this, those days where my body and mind combined to provide me with the faith and cool head needed to lead a challenging climb, are the ones that linger in my memory. It is an amazing place to be; moving with confidence up an exposed rock face, climbing free and feeling free. The exhilaration is very special.

I always found that I climbed better with some people than others. By 'climbed better' I don't just mean my technical skills were better; in fact I don't think I mean that at all. Over the years there were so many routes on which I backed off from the lead, not because I was not strong or skilled enough to climb them, but because my head was not in the right place. While the person you climb with is not responsible for your own state of mind while climbing, I found that some people helped me to find the mindset I required to have confidence in my own abilities, to be able to lead a pitch without the self-doubt that is so mentally draining.

I had not climbed very much with Nirvana but she was one of those people for me, and I think I was the same for her. Over the years I spent climbing, I think I could probably count on one hand the people with which I felt this level of compatibility and understanding that so helped me to push myself to climb at my best.

A Dream of White Horses — or *Dream* — is known amongst climbers as an easy climb in an extraordinary situation. A rising traverse of the gaping chasm of Wen Zawn; five rope lengths of exhilarating and well-protected climbing. Graded HVS, *Dream* is not strenuous or technical for the grade; its main difficulties lie in the exposure of the route and in the committing nature of the climb. Once started it is hard to escape, the only real option being to reverse the route to its starting point and climb up an easier chimney.

After we had finished climbing *The Ramp*, we agreed that we should then go for the main reason we had come to Gogarth: to climb *A Dream of White Horses*. Our approach to the climb was to abseil down the right-hand side of Wen Zawn to the start of the route.

We had looked at the route from the clifftop on the other side of the zawn. Wen Slab was itself impressive, clean and creamy grey in colour. You could make out the line of the climb, a series of cracks that rise on a diagonal from the bottom right to around three quarters of the way up the left-hand side of the slab — about 100 metres in length. From here the route traverses leftwards across the lip of the zawn, eventually to the clifftop and the end of the climb.

While it looked like the climbing on this last pitch would be straightforward, the exposure would be something else; look down from that pitch and all you would see beneath your feet would be air and the sea 50 metres or so beneath your feet.

I led off on the first pitch. The climbing was straightforward and there was plenty of protection. I enjoyed the feeling of moving across the rock. The route is one of the most popular on Gogarth and is very well travelled — the climb was clean, with no loose rock or slimy bits to contend with. The sea was not far below but it was very calm, no real swell or spray to bother us. A couple of sea-kayakers paddled by; we waved and exchanged greetings as they explored the cliffs from a different perspective.

I finished the pitch and set up the belay — the point at which the leader stops climbing and anchors themselves to the rock, enabling them to bring up the second safely. If the second falls while climbing the belay holds their weight. When climbing, the second removes all of the protection placed on the pitch by the leader, so leaving the rock as it was found. This is the nature of traditional climbing, the alternative being sport climbing, where bolts are drilled permanently into the rock and used by the leader as points of protection.

When climbing a route with multiple pitches, sharing the lead — where each climber takes it in turns to lead a pitch — is both efficient and smooth. Each is tied in to opposing ends of the rope. It is important to keep the rope free of tangles and knots and sharing the lead helps to keep the rope organised. It can also be useful mentally. When a climber has led a particularly hard or scary pitch, it can be a relief to know they can have a break; that all they have to do next is second.

Having completed the first pitch, Nirvana moved through to lead the second. I sensed that she was a little nervous but still confident in her climbing. This was the first day she had climbed on sea cliffs. She moved smoothly and calmly, placing protection at good intervals. This next pitch looked like great climbing; good handholds with less for the feet. Smearing — using the friction of our sticky rubber climbing shoes on the rock — was required.

I watched Nirvana attentively; if she fell I would need to react very quickly to hold her fall. My mind wandered. I remember thinking to myself that I had been lucky that summer to climb on some brilliant sea cliffs in the UK — in Dorset, Cornwall, Pembrokeshire and now Gogarth. Each were different — the steep, juggy, fossilised walls of Boulder Ruckle at Swanage, the slabby granite cliffs of Bosigran, the sharp limestone of Bosherton Head and now the famous Wen Zawn. I felt quite comfortable with where we were and what we were doing. I was glad that my head was familiar with sea cliffs and the added air of fear that climbing above the sea can bring.

Nirvana finished climbing and set up a hanging belay; literally hung off the cliff held by the protection she had placed to make her safe at the belay. I began seconding the pitch as she coiled the rope across the cradle formed by her legs and the cliff face. As there became more rope to manage, it started to fall from her legs and drop down, becoming tangled and knotted. I paused as she focused on trying to sort the rope out. The tangles were getting worse, and then she managed to drop some kit from her harness.

The karabiner made a hollow 'plop' sound as it hit the water beneath us. A wave of realisation and vertigo suddenly washed over me.

That sea is real. These cliffs are no place for me — what am I doing here? All it takes is one slip and it could be me hitting the water and quickly sinking as all of my climbing ironmongery drags me down. I felt exposed and, while she was a rope's length away from me, I knew Nirvana was uneasy too. I felt like I was losing control.

The trick with climbing in such places is to turn off the part of your brain that alerts you to the danger you should usually associate with that situation. If you climb enough, you become numbed to this alert, so accustomed to the exposure formed by height, space and location that it's normal. Right there, paused halfway up *Dream*, these places were very normal for me. Hanging around on high mountain crags and sea cliffs formed a regular part of my weekend escapes from urbanity. That a falling piece of climbing gear, dropped by my climbing partner, broke this state of mind for me was telling. The sound of the karabiner hitting the sea was all it took.

Although we did not talk about it, both of us felt the same. While we were not in any immediate danger, we had both stopped suppressing those thoughts and emotions that, if focused on, would lead you to never go climbing in the first place. Some would say that these thoughts are reality-based, others that they are fear-based. Either way, they are not helpful when halfway along a challenging and exposed multi-pitched rock climb.

We collected our thoughts and Nirvana sorted out the rope. We pressed on to climb the third pitch and quickly reached the belay stance in the chimney formed by the corner of Wen Slab and the opposing upper wall of the zawn.

Late afternoon. The air was growing heavy; cloudier and darker. That late-summer feeling of a brewing thunderstorm. In other circumstances this can be a cause for concern. Rain at Wimbledon stops play and a heavy shower can spoil an evening barbecue. This time the feeling filled me with fear. The weather and our mood felt foreboding. We still had the last pitch to complete before we could get off the cliff and away.

This pitch is probably the easiest to climb, with big holds for both your hands and feet.

'A fall from the final pitch would leave a climber hanging free 70 metres above the sea.'

These words from the route description in the Gogarth guidebook resonated through my mind. Easy climbing but don't fall off or you'll be hanging free in the chasm that forms Wen Zawn.

We moved quickly to begin the last pitch. My lead.

Normally in climbing, leading is more serious and committing than seconding. As the rope will generally be above the second's head, if they fall as they climb, the rope will immediately hold them. But the sideways climbing nature of a traverse like *Dream* means that the norm is not the case; pitches like this are as serious for the second as they are the leader. We were both fairly psyched, and I was glad I had the lead as it meant that I got it over with first; I didn't have to mull it over at the belay stance while the leader climbed. In the back of my head there was another, more selfish, reason: finishing the route first meant I had less chance of having to climb this exposed final pitch in heavy rain.

I stepped across on to the lip of the zawn — instant exposure. The foot and handholds were big enough to feel very comfortable on, but it was the huge expanse of air directly below me that gave me discomfort. Climbing on the arch of the zawn, looking down between my legs I could see white spray crashing against the lower cliff. Easy climbing, but in an extraordinary situation!

Looking to my left I could see the line I had to follow. Clear holds were there for my hands and for my feet. If this traverse was just inches above stable ground, I think I could probably have done it blindfolded, on feel alone. Yet here, it felt much harder. I continued, trying not to look down, not to think about what I was doing and what a fall here would mean. I focussed on the moves — hold to hold — the actions my body had to complete to take itself across the cliff.

I reached the grassy clifftop at the end of the traverse and was safe — attached to the belay I had established. Nirvana began climbing and she soon reached me and the clifftop.

The climb was over. A brilliant route and we had enjoyed it tremendously. It is strange looking back to remember how such an inconsequential thing as dropping a karabiner in the sea brought on such fear. I suppose this shows just how fickle a state of mind can be: one minute immune to place, the next having to suppress growing feelings of panic.

The first heavy drops of rain started to fall ten minutes after we topped out, as we headed over to find our friends who had retreated earlier from the sea cliffs to the less fearsome, more relaxed crags on the side of Holyhead mountain.

Sea cliff climbing is always an amazing experience. It is elemental. The combination of the beauty of a rugged coastline, the wild exposure on the rock face and the constant, menacing, presence of the sea always left me wanting to come back for more. Don't get me wrong, I have had some of my scariest moments in these places, it's just that over time most of these tend to get forgotten. Instead I remember those moments of pure exhilaration that adorn the other side of the same coin.

FOUR

MOUNTAIN MARATHON 2

A year after our first foray into the hills on a mountain marathon, The Wolf and I were back on the start line. This time the KIMM was being held in the hills to the north of Kielder reservoir in Northumberland. We were about as far north in England as we could go. In fact over the course of the weekend we would cross over the border into Scotland as we ran across the fells.

The weather was a touch better than the previous year, and the going slightly easier underfoot. We were again running the C course, but this time we were familiar with the format of the event, and so were able to focus on the running rather than first having to try and work out what was going on.

By now The Wolf and I had been sharing a house for over a year and we knew one another better. There are not many people I knew then or know now that I would count as such a friend as her. Over the previous summer, together with our housemates and other friends from the university climbing club, we had been drawn more closely together by the deaths of Dom and Arne. While these friendships were — and still are — a great thing, in the months succeeding that summer, they were also very intense. Combined with the work The Wolf and I were both having to do in the final year of our undergraduate courses, this weekend running around unfamiliar hills trying to find ourselves in the right places (or perhaps that should be trying not to get lost) was something I think we both found to be a good way of letting off steam.

Since our first mountain marathon I had done very little in the way of learning to read a map, so the map I was handed at the start was again more or less useless. Like the year before, I again followed The Wolf, who herself had improved a bit, probably due to mapping fieldwork for her Geology degree in the Alps the previous summer.

Over the weekend the weather worsened but it was never as bad as the year before. While the upland we were running over felt remote, it was relatively easy going compared to the seemingly endless tussocks of the Galloway Hills. With less drama (from both ourselves and the conditions) we finished our course, placing about halfway through the field.

Putting aside the fact that I had nothing at all to do with the navigation over the weekend it had been pretty straightforward really. It was time to make it a bit more difficult.

The year after I was keen to do a B course. The Wolf wasn't all that interested in this — I think she was happy to do the C course. She had also started a Masters degree in Surrey, was focused on her studies and could not get to the hills so easily to train from where she was based. I had stayed in Leeds after graduating, and had more or less gone straight from finishing my degree into work. While I didn't really know what I wanted to do, I applied for a job as a trainee software programmer for a company in Wakefield, and was very surprised when I was offered it after an interview I thought I had completely messed up.

Starting to work for a living after the relative freedom of study was a real shock to my system. When I was fourteen I had worked in a newsagent at the weekends, staying there until I left Bristol to go to university, and after that occasionally working hours when I was back home at Christmas and in the summer. I was used to having to get up early and working in order to gain a disposable income. It wasn't the discipline needed to get out of bed that was the problem. What was the problem was that I could see an end to the job in the paper shop, but a real job earning the money I needed to live and continue to have adventures spanned decades into my future, far longer than I had already lived. Moreover, as soon as I started working, I began an intensive three-month training programme during which time I would learn — from scratch — the programming language I would be working in, and also how to apply it in the situations my employers required. I found the combination of having to succeed (I found the training course difficult conceptually at first. I was on probation and if I failed would lose my job) and coping with the fact that this nine-to-five life was something I was going to have to do for most of the rest of my days pretty stressful. For a while I would often arrive home on a Tuesday evening and have a little weep — it was such a long time until the weekend and such a long time until I could retire.

Having just finished the KIMM in 1996 with Ellen Wolfenden. *Photo: Ellen Wolfenden collection*

It did not take me too long to settle into understanding programming and software development, and the routine of working five days a week. I figured I had to do it so I might as well get used to it, and I soon learned that working full-time forces you to become better at using your time — I could still do loads of other things if I did not waste time.

After my three-month probationary period my employers unleashed me on the world of real work. And it was very real — lots of scope for learning, problem solving, innovating and making associated mistakes. Looking back now I was so green — so many things to learn. I am sure I will reflect on myself ten or so years from now and think the same. I wonder (who knows) where I will be then.

During this intense period of learning it was a relief to have something completely different to focus on. I found it really refreshing. I had started working in the late summer of 1998, about the same time I started to up my preparation towards the B class KIMM in October. Weekends were spent heading to the mountains to rock climb and I began to inter-space the climbing with running in the hills.

As The Wolf was not up for it I needed a new partner. Aidan fitted the bill nicely; he could navigate pretty well and went for the odd run now and then. We had been together for almost two years and were now living together in a friend's attic room in Leeds 6, just around the corner from the house I had shared with The Wolf, Sarah, Kate and a host of others. Our training consisted of evening runs up the Meanwood Valley Trail after work and weekend trips away to the Lakes, North Wales and the Peak District.

We had even started to do the odd fell race — Al Powell gave us lifts to them in the back of his Astra van. Our first fell race that autumn was the Three Shires race in the Lake District. It felt as hard as hell, not helped by the fact that we arrived at the start in Little Langdale ten minutes after the race had started and were therefore playing catch-up all the way around. Given that I would have been towards the back of the field even if I had started with it, chasing desperately up the first hill, trying to work out where to go was tough going and rather disheartening. I also remember running off the second from last hill thinking I was running to the finish, only to be presented with the final tough climb and a feeling of wonderment: would I be able to do it? I did, and the pie at the finish tasted all the better for it.

After the next fell race, the classic Langdale Horseshoe in early October, I felt ready for the B class KIMM. I had never done so much preparation for a race and neither had Aidan; surely we would succeed. The race that year was being held in the Howgill fells. These hills are in Cumbria, on the western edge of the Yorkshire Dales, and are far quieter than their neighbouring fells in the Lake District. These are grassy fells, with tops linked by high ridges and separated by steep valleys. I think they are some of the best hills for running in England. For those familiar with the history of the KIMM, they are also infamous for the event that became known as the 'Howling Howgills' due to the appalling weather experienced over the weekend, and particularly on the Saturday. It was this event that Aidan and I had been training towards.

We were one of the last pairs to start the race on the Saturday morning, with a start time of nearly 10 a.m. We had travelled over the evening before, as usual in the back of Al Powell's van. Al was going for the Elite win with his brother Ifor.

The weather was just horrible, lashing rain and strong winds. In any normal situation you would not consider going out into the hills in such conditions, it would just be too grim. As Aidan and I sat in Al's van awaiting our time to start, we wondered why some pairs were walking back from the start line. The penny dropped: these guys were dropping out of the event before they had even started. The weather was that bad. I understood why they were not racing but I was still determined that we would start and fortunately so was Aidan.

I have never run at such an angle. As we ran along the ridge up towards our second checkpoint it was necessary to lean far in to the wind blasting across me just to stay upright. When we got to the checkpoint at the top of Docker Knoll we had had to crawl on hands and knees to clip it otherwise we may have been blown away down the hill.

Throughout the day we progressed but it was very slow going. The navigation was not too tricky but the weather was so incessantly bad and impeded anything faster than a walk. We were always fighting the strong wind and it was all we could do to see where we were going given the rain driving into our faces. About two-thirds of the way to the overnight campsite we had a road crossing. Our route then headed towards and around Wild Boar Fell and Mallerstang Edge, before dropping into the valley and the day's finish.

We sort of knew that we had no hope of making the checkpoint cut-off times, and if we did not we would be disqualified. So what was the point of going on? I was frustrated that as we had one of the latest start times we were impeded from the start — others would have had an extra two hours on the hill before the checkpoints closed. The organisers had a shuttle bus running from the road crossing back to the event centre and it was just too tempting to get in — so, frustrated, tired and soaked, we retired from the race. As we clambered into the bus a cracking bolt of lightning tore from the sky, followed by a large clap of thunder. It felt like an omen.

We weren't alone in retiring that day. In the B course alone over two thirds of people either did not start or quit the race part way through the first day. That did not stop me being really pissed off — we had failed.

In the years to come the reputation the Howling Howgills had of being the worst weather OMM ever would be superseded by Borrowdale in 2008. I learned a lot from that weekend — about coping with such bad weather conditions and that sometimes all the training in the world cannot control an outcome if what gets thrown at you by nature overrides this control. Funnily enough it was years before I went back to the Howgills, yet nowadays they are one of my favourite stretch of hills.

My next attempt at a B course had rather more success — in the summer of 2000 I ran the Lowe Alpine Mountain Marathon with my friend Rich. Aidan had been too busy with his exams before the LAMM to train (or at least that is what he had claimed). Rich was a good friend of Al's which is how we had met.

Yet again I got into the back of Al's Astra van to be driven from the middle of Leeds to some mountains. This time we were heading to the Black Mount — the hills in the southern Highlands of Scotland that lie in between and to the west of the Glens of Orchy and Etive. The LAMM is always held in the Scottish Highlands in June. I had been up that way before but only to winter climb in Glencoe and on Ben Nevis; the other mountains around there were a complete mystery to me.

And that mystery remained for the whole of the weekend. I did not read the map at all. Rich was OK at navigation but clearly found it very challenging in the thick misty conditions we experienced on the Sunday. That is not a criticism as all I did was follow him uselessly, hoping that we were going in the right direction. I remember the shared relief we felt at finding the last but one checkpoint on Sunday afternoon — we had been looking for it for ages. All we had to do from there was run off the hill towards the finish, finding a final checkpoint along the way.

Of the thousand or so competitors who raced the LAMM, Rich and I were just about flat last off the hill. It had taken us hours but we had finished the B course. It had been tough going — my feet were shredded — but we were still very pleased with ourselves, despite the fact that many other runners would be south of Glasgow on their ways back home by the time we got to the finish. Al must have had to wait hours for us. He and Ifor had won the Elite, their second win at the LAMM. True to his nature Al didn't complain about waiting for us, but congratulated us and, after our enquiries and with a little smile on his face, quietly told us he had won.

FIVE

CAR CRASH

As the car hit me I was thrown backwards, over the top of it, and landed in the oncoming lane. The only noise I remember is Richard's urgent shouting of my name. He was shouting for me to get out of the road. I scrabbled into the thin lay-bay alongside the road. There was no pain; it came later. I checked I could still wiggle my toes and then lay back to wait for the ambulance. My memory of these moments is precise and crisp, almost mechanistic.

I recall my next thought vividly.

'I am alive.'

An overwhelming sense of relief flooded through me, followed by an amazing sense of awareness.

'Nothing else matters.'

The only thing I cared about in that moment was my life. The importance of the material vanished; I was left with a need — an immense, irrepressible urge — for survival and fulfilment.

It was two days before Christmas, 2000 — a Saturday — almost a year to the day since Aidan and I had moved out of Leeds 6, to Otley, where together we had bought a house. The day had started for me with a slight hangover and the last of my Christmas shopping. Leaving it even later than me, Aidan had driven into Leeds to do all of his.

Rich had called and we arranged to go mountain biking on the Otley Chevin that afternoon.

The Chevin is steep wooded hillside that forms a forest park above Otley, the market town ten or so miles north-west of Leeds. Otley sits in Wharfedale, a valley that begins in the heart of the Yorkshire Dales and opens out to the east, where the two rivers Wharfe and Ouse meet on the plain near York. Otley itself is a town of typical Yorkshire character. Its position is a great one; to the south are the industrial and populous valleys of the Aire and the Calder, capped on their high edges by rugged moor. To the north and west the emptier valleys of the Washburn, Nidd, Ribble, Ure and Swale; rivers that between them form the Yorkshire Dales. The closeness of the cities of Leeds and Bradford ensure that employment is relatively plentiful but far enough away to be easily escaped. Whenever I crest the top of the Leeds road on my way home, Wharfedale opens out in front of me, with Otley nestled close by on the valley floor. It is always a welcome view.

Great for running, biking and home to the famous Caley crags, the Chevin is a brilliant place to have on the doorstep. It is riddled with great paths and trails, with some of the best singletrack I know. Coupled with the superb gritstone boulders that form one of the best places for bouldering in the UK, along with two grit edges offering fine rock climbing routes, the Chevin is a great playground, both by day and by night.

From Otley, the Leeds road makes a rising traverse up the east side of the Chevin. At around 2 p.m. I cycled up the road away from Otley with Rich behind me. It was a typical mid-winter day that had started with freezing fog and had stayed much the same. Throughout the day the fog had steadily thinned but was still lingering in places, in particular clinging in layers to the pine trees of the forest.

I was hoping for one of those crispy winter rides, where the normally wet and muddy ground is frozen. On the crispiest of these days, riding is comparable to a dry and dusty summer trail, made better still by the winter sun sitting low in the sky, enhancing the light and colours. While the sun had not materialised, the ground was frozen solid, and we were looking forward to a blast around the forest.

I had done this ride around my local trails many times before. It was like any other normal Saturday afternoon. Normality: is it worth my while? Behaving in a routine fashion can be stifling and lead to boredom and the mundane. Do I waste my time with the normal, should I always strive for the unusual, the extraordinary? Maybe I should be more appreciative of those normal and ordinary things that are so enabling.

I spend a great deal of time on the Chevin. Much of my training time; hill-reps and speed sessions. Rides into work; over the top of the hill and then the back roads into Leeds. Night runs in the winter, escaping into the darkness after work. Descending smooth trails surrounded by bluebells in the spring. The odd bouldering session on a warm evening, trying to remember the 'Caley knack' that allows you to climb those delicate problems with seemingly no effort. And, perhaps the best, early morning runs and rides, just me and the deer, traversing dewy singletrack, preparing my mind and body for the day ahead. I am so lucky that all of these things are ordinary, and this is something I sometimes forget.

Something extraordinary happened to me that Saturday afternoon. Turning right, onto the trail from the Leeds road, I was hit by a car at 50 miles per hour.

Lying in the lay-by my mind wandered. I felt little pain but I knew I had been hit hard. Broken bones? Not sure. Would I still be able to walk? These things and other worse scenarios were entirely possible, and I do not write these words flippantly, or without full appreciation of the situation I had put myself in. The overwhelming feeling I had was that, whatever injuries and their effects on my life, the most important thing is that I was alive. Fate, luck, chance, had been with me, it could have finished so much differently. I was changed from that moment. I still had my life. That is everything.

I do not believe in a god. Each of us is only here for a brief time. Part of why I find contentment when high in the mountains is because I find their age, their relatively infinite nature, reassuring. I am just a flash in the pan compared to the Cumbrian fells or the jagged, snow-capped Alps. I don't find that a depressing thought. While the mountains remind me of my mortality and fallibility, they also put my fears and worries into context. The stark reality that strikes me when surrounded by beautiful towering peaks is that nothing really matters. This serves to remind me to make the best of everything, enjoy the moment, indulge the good and forget the bad. I'm only around for the blink of an eye. Make it count.

Our instinct for survival drives us to pass our genes on to our children and the next generation. But what about the life we lead? There is fulfilment to be found in so many places, and it is this fulfilment that I continually seek. This search can be risky. Failure has many forms. Loss, premature end, injury, death. Sometimes the proximity of failing is obvious. A climber on a rock face, high above the last placed protection, legs shaking wildly with fatigue and fear, stares it in the face. At times failure can surprise you. That Saturday afternoon it rushed up and caught me by surprise. Complacency. Never forget what you have, how great living is. The bad times can be truly terrible. Getting through them makes you stronger and serves to give a means of comparison. If there were no bad times how would we know good?

The ambulance arrived and took me to the Leeds General Infirmary. The last Saturday before Christmas, the place was full of very drunk people. I did not notice this or the noise and trouble they were making. I had quickly been given morphine and was in my own little world of suppressed pain. It felt like I was there for only two hours but actually it was more like 15. After X-rays, that revealed nothing was broken, I waited for a doctor to be available who could sew up the big cuts on the back of my right arm. It was my right side that had taken the impact; I had damage to my leg, torso, shoulder and arm.

It was funny that Chris, the doctor who stitched me up, was a cyclist and runner. He knew a fair few of my running friends and lived in Leeds 6, in the same house as Al Powell. Six months later Chris and I would meet again, in a pub in Otley after a fell race, where I showed him the scars on my arm and we both admired his handiwork.

After the stitches and other patching up, I was allowed to go home. Christmas passed in a concussed blur. I can remember Boxing Day, lying on my sofa, drifting in and out of sleep listening to Radio 4 as Stephen Fry read the first Harry Potter book in its entirety. The day after I tried sitting up some more. Our housemate Colin had purloined a wheelchair from Safeway over the road and he and Aidan took turns pushing me through Otley, to our local pub the Bowling Green, where I enjoyed a half.

Over the next few days I was walking more and more. I had taken a big knock to my lower leg, and one of the nurses in Wharfedale hospital, where I went for wound redressing and painkillers, said the tissue damage looked like an outline of the Isle of Wight. The scar still does today.

On New Year's Day, we parked close to Beamsley Beacon, in the eastern Dales near Bolton Abbey. A crisp sunny day and a dusting of snow; renewal was in the air for me. I stumbled up and down the hillside. Although in a lot of pain, it felt so good to be outside somewhere beautiful. My body was working; my fears immediately after the crash had not borne out. I was literally full of resolution for the year ahead, and the years beyond that. Seize the day, the challenges and the opportunities. They are there to be risen to and achieved.

I steadily recovered and built my fitness back up. Some of my injuries recovered quicker than others. My leg took a while to heal — at one stage they discussed a skin graft. Fortunately this was not necessary; it slowly healed to form the Isle of Wight scar I have today. I had a pocket of fluid in my right bum cheek that became infected in early February.

Half my arse swelled to twice its size and I had to go back into hospital for intravenous antibiotics. It got better and I was left with a large solid haematoma in its place. My right bicep was at first completely floppy and then withered away in less than two months. I also had no sensation in my right forearm or hand. The doctors thought this was caused by nerve damage that occurred when my shoulder took a lot of the impact from the crash. The nerve was squashed and no longer had the ability to contract or stimulate my bicep and so the muscle wasted. Again, after tests they spoke of surgery but decided against it — the nerve would eventually mend itself. It did and now, while my forearm is still numb, I have a working bicep.

During all this recovery time, it was perhaps ironic that, given the cause of my injuries had been bike related, the only sport I did was cycling. I could not climb because of my arm and shoulder and I could not run because of my leg and arse. Prior to the crash my main focus was climbing and afterwards it was most definitely cycling.

Nine months after the accident, in August 2001, I rode the Grand Raid mountain bike race in Switzerland. This is a fearsome event in the Valais region that covers an off-road route of 130 kilometres, with 3500 metres of ascent. Starting in the ski resort of Verbier, it crosses three valleys and mountain passes, including the infamous Pas de Lona, to finish in Grimentz. It was by far the hardest physical challenge I had attempted and I almost didn't make it to the start line. There are timing cut-offs throughout the race. If you don't make them you are forcibly retired and get transported to the finish in a bus. I did not want this to happen to me, although it was entirely possible given the difficulty of the route and the fact that I had never ridden such big climbs before. I allowed myself to get psyched out — I listened too much to people I knew who had completed the Grand Raid before and who were full of bravado and doubt. I believed them too much and almost lost my own self-belief.

It was a beautiful day. The race started at 6 a.m. and, as we left Verbier heading north-east, I allowed myself to take a look back over my shoulder at the pink glow of the sunrise on the Suisse Aiguilles. The riding was superb — amazing trails and singletrack that traversed steep mountainsides, with breathtaking Alpine scenery. The fear of failure steadily abated as I progressed through the day and I made the last timing gate with an hour to spare. I was so pleased that even the 45-minute bike carry up the scree slope that forms the col of the Pas de Lona seemed fantastic. At 3000 metres the air was thin and I was tired, but the spectators cheered me and every other knackered rider on. From the top all that was left was an awesome 20-kilometre descent down to Grimentz. An amazing day and some lessons learned. Just because it is hard does not make it impossible and a challenge is made all the harder if you do not believe you can do it.

Writing this nine years later I am recovering from another bike crash. Will it be the last? It happened in the Outer Hebrides, on the island of Harris, the most mountainous of these Western Isles. Its hills are rocky and rough, and the going is hard underfoot. But this difficulty is more than recompensed by their beauty.

There is a road that hugs the eastern coastline of the island. Rising and falling with the land, it travels through a beautiful, rugged landscape and is called 'The Golden Road'. With my bike I had taken a ferry from Berneray on North Uist to Leverburgh on the south end of Harris. I was planning to cycle along the Golden Road and further, returning later to Leverburgh and back to North Uist.

Although it was a windy day, I was thankful it was not raining as it had done persistently for the previous few days. The Western Isles are amazing islands. Situated off the north-west coast of Scotland, they are a journey away and feel as such. With the sun and a gentle breeze they are utterly beautiful. As the locals are all keen to tell you this doesn't happen every day.

The islands are strewn with hills and lochans. On the east side of the islands, away from the spine of the main road that takes you the length of the islands, the land quickly becomes wild; untrodden and remote. Rugged and mountainous, boggy and unforgiving, you can wander for miles without seeing anybody, or any path or footprints that give previous presence away.

Over the years I had spent quite some time on South Uist. My aunt was a doctor on the islands and has a croft in Loch Aineort on the west of South Uist, directly south of the stretch of the three island peaks of Hecla, Beinn Corradail and Beinn Mhor. I had also spent a week travelling the length of the islands, from Barra in the south, across South Uist, Benbecula, North Uist and Harris to Lewis, competing the Hebridean Challenge adventure race.

Having spent just a brief time on Harris, I was hankering to return and this road ride was an opportunity to explore it some more. I caught the early morning ferry, and had been cycling for just under an hour. I had planned a steady ride — five hours or so — on the lovely, lonely, swoopy roads, basking in the scenery and with the odd stop for a cup of tea. How quickly things can change.

Taking it easy, following the road as it descended towards the sea, holding the line around the bend. Except I didn't hold the line. Gravel under my rear wheel threw me offline, I lost control.

It all happened so quickly.

This stretch of road is raised up, with big drops on both sides down steep boulder strewn banks. Suddenly, I was heading at speed off the road. I tried to recover but failed. I was off, on a lightweight carbon road bike that was no match for big rocks, especially at speed. The last thing that went through my head before I hit the rocks was 'this is going to hurt'.

It did. I landed on my back, winded, on a patch of grass 20 metres or so down the bank. With blood dripping from my head, I turned to look at my bike. It had snapped clean in two. Survival quickly took hold.

Worried I might pass out, I scrambled back up to the road and sat by the side of it, my head in my hands, trying to breathe normally and keep the steady stream of blood out of my eyes. If I had blacked out where I landed, no one would have found me. I sat by the road and waited for the next car. It seemed like an age. Long enough to think despairingly and question why it had happened again. Long enough to think about telling Aidan and the worry I would cause him and the rest of my family. Long enough to be thankful.

Again, the ordinary had turned into the extraordinary. All it had taken was some grit under my rear wheel and I was down. It could have been so much worse. Despite a big cut to my forehead, badly swollen knees and right shoulder, perhaps a broken wrist and big bruises all over the front of my body, I was OK. Equally, I'd had some bad luck. In plenty of other situations, on skidding off a road, I would have a soft landing in a hedgerow or verge, with nothing to speak of except slight embarrassment at my own incompetence.

The next car arrived, with a driver and passenger. They gently helped me into the front seat and insisted on recovering my bike. They put it in the boot, into which it fitted easily in its newly foldable state.

For the rest of the day I sampled some of the healthcare facilities on the Western Isles. I was dropped off at the GP surgery in Tarbet, about ten miles from where I had crashed. They patched me up and, suspecting a dislocated shoulder, packed me and my bike off to Stornaway in an ambulance.

On the Isle of Lewis, Stornaway is the capital of the Western Isles and is by far the largest town. I had been there once before and, compared to the rest of the townships on the islands, it is a sprawling metropolis, with traffic lights, housing estates and all the other things that together constitute some people's definition of 'civilisation'. Around 60-percent of the whole of the islands' population live there. I find it amazing that everywhere else on the Western Isles is so very different to suburban normality. Depending on how you look at it, Stornaway is a bizarre anomaly or a breath of fresh air. Despite my own opinion that Stornaway is the former, it was personally very useful that it had another trapping of urban life — a general hospital.

The staff were kind. I was trolleyed through to A&E, where they arranged for X-rays to my shoulder, torso and wrist. No fractures or dislocations were revealed, so they gave me some strong painkillers and I was allowed to leave. My broken bike and I took a taxi back to Leverburgh, where Aidan met me to escort me back to North Uist. A wrecked holiday but the relief to us both was palpable.

Another reminder of my mortality and fallibility. Will it be the last? Should I quit it all and stay safe? And what about Aidan? The distress and anxiety my accidents put him through are the hardest things to cope with. As I lay in the lay-by on the Leeds road, I was aware that some other car drivers had stopped to find out what they could do to help. I could hear their voices, but wasn't paying much attention to what was being said. Suddenly, there was a voice I recognised, edged with fear and panic. Aidan. Driving home in a car full of Christmas presents, he had seen me and stopped.

At first he didn't know whether I was alive or dead. How can that have felt? The desperate feeling of seeing someone you love on the ground and not knowing how they are. Rich reassured him and then I spoke to him. He came with me in the ambulance to hospital. In the weeks after the accident we acknowledged that its impact on him psychologically was at least as great as the impact on me. I still have dreams where I jump awake at night, feeling the car as it hits me. Aidan has to handle memories of the deep distress caused by seeing me on the ground after the crash, and at first he found it hard to reconcile that I should cycle again.

There is a real selfishness here. The mountaineer Alison Hargreaves was chastised by a large proportion of the British press for leaving her two young children and husband behind as she went climbing. She died on K2. There was a sexism to the reportage and also a sense of bewilderment.

People could not understand why a mother would choose to leave her family and attempt a mountain as fierce and as dangerous as K2. While these people may have also questioned a man's decision to do the same thing, it is far more acceptable in society for this to happen.

In my mind, this selfishness is not driven by a desire to be cruel, to be better than anyone, or to win, but by a need to really feel alive. The perversity is that this feeling is at its most intense when — deliberately or otherwise — you get closer to death.

PART 2

LEARNING

Flowerdale

SIX

MOUNTAIN MARATHON 3

Quite a few years passed before I ran another mountain marathon. The injuries I sustained when hit by the car on the Leeds road at first impeded my ability to run and, by the time I could run again, I was so focused on cycling that it was all I really did, running only occasionally around the Chevin and during lunch breaks at work. Instead of mountain marathons and fell races I raced on two wheels at similar events.

The Polaris Challenge is the mountain bike equivalent of a mountain marathon. At its peak of popularity it would take place three times a year, in March, July and October, and around a thousand people would ride the event. I rode loads of them, in the Lake District, Peak District, Northern Pennines, Exmoor, the Isle of Man, Mid-Wales, the Scottish Borders and the Yorkshire Dales. I chased the win and eventually got it, after a steep learning curve, at the 2003 event at Easter on the Isle of Man — an amazing place to go mountain biking.

I rode in different countries, in particular the Alpine regions. The Grand Raid Cristalp and the eight-day Transalp mountain bike races, the Etape du Tour and La Marmotte road cyclosportives were some of the classic events I endured and enjoyed. Back in the UK I rode the Fred Whitton cyclosportive five times, and became even more obsessed with the wonderful Three Peaks Cyclo-Cross.

One of the things with mountain biking in the UK, in particular England and Wales, is that you rarely get to the top of a hill. As it is not legal to ride on footpaths, riders are restricted to bridleways and byways. While there are many, many great trails to ride, as these tracks are often the remnants of old packhorse roads they rarely summit hills but take the line of least resistance across them, forming the link as they did in the past between two or more dwelling places, villages or towns.

So, while I love mountain biking for the places I can go on my mountain bike — both the beautiful and the thrilling as I ride through mountainous scenery along challenging trails — and for the journeys you can go on, it got to the point that it wasn't enough: I wanted to get to the tops of hills too. This was the reason I started fell running again in early 2004.

Unlike me, Aidan had never really stopped running. He loved mammoth runs in the hills. For quite a while he had been training over the Bob Graham Round — the legendary 65-mile route in the Lake District that summits 42 peaks and that fell runners challenge themselves to complete in under 24 hours. However, during these runs he kept trashing his ankles, turning and spraining them with unfortunate regularity. We entered the Old County Tops fell race together — a 37-mile fell race run in pairs that climbs the three highest peaks of the old Lake District counties of Westmorland, Cumberland and Lancashire. I had entered with Aidan with some trepidation — while I was by then used to long days out, they were on my bike, not my feet. The race started outside the New Dungeon Ghyll Hotel in Great Langdale, heading over a low shoulder of the Langdale Pikes to Grasmere, up Helvellyn, across to Scafell Pike and then down the wonderful Upper Eskdale to cross onto the Old Man of Coniston range of hills at Cockley Beck, up the Old Man and then back to Great Langdale. It was a beautiful sunny day in the middle of May, and the race started at 8 a.m. Within half an hour Aidan had turned his bad ankle, and after about ten miles we had to retire from the race as he was in too much pain to continue. More frustration, but when someone is injured it is pretty daft to carry on and risk making it a lot worse.

By June Aidan's ankle had recovered enough for us to enter the LAMM together. That year it was being held in the Trossachs, the forest and mountains largely situated around Ben Lomond, the most southerly of Scotland's Munros. We did not want to be overambitious and so entered the C course. The organisers transported us from the event centre to the start across Loch Katrine on a steamboat; from the deck of the boat — the Sir Walter Scott — we watched the hills we would soon be running over glide by serenely.

We started and headed for the first checkpoint. Rushing around we could not find it. We slowed down, still could not find it, and were confused by a checkpoint for a different course being very close to where we believed ours should be. After a long while we decided that the first checkpoint was not in the correct place and pressed on to checkpoint two. We soon found it and made good progress to the rest throughout the day. When we arrived at the campsite we immediately enquired about the location of the first checkpoint, and that we thought it must have been placed incorrectly. Everyone else had found it so this was not the case — it was us in the wrong, not the checkpoint.

While we were disappointed we weren't really all that surprised; we hadn't given ourselves enough time to think on the start line, we just ran off in what we thought was roughly the right direction. Although missing out a checkpoint means automatic disqualification, we ran the second day's course and managed to complete it: it was good practice — practice that we needed.

Figuring we couldn't get that much worse at finding the first check-point of a mountain marathon, Aidan and I entered the following autumn's KIMM together, that year held in the Cheviots, and this time running the B course.

To cut to the chase we ran up the wrong hill from the start and it took us well over an hour to work out what we had done wrong. We had one of the latest start times and so after an error of this scale were never going to get back on track and finish the course before it closed and darkness fell. We retired and went home with our tails well and truly between our legs. Again, from the start line we had run off like headless chickens. Amazingly each of us ran past a series of farm buildings as we climbed the hill on which we both thought the first checkpoint was, and silently thought, 'It's funny that that farm is not on the map.'

Of course it was on the map — we were running up the wrong hill and were in a different place on the ground than we thought on the map! I can smile about this now, but at the time it made me crazy — why could we not complete these things? Why could we not even properly start these things?

It did not take much analysis for us to realise that we both found getting to the first checkpoint difficult. That it takes the brain a little while to become in-tune with the unfamiliar map and surroundings is not all that surprising really. The irony is that, while on one side the brain needs to be slow and methodical, the race situation makes another side of it scream for speed. There is a middle ground somewhere between the two, which itself gets closer to the speed side the more experienced and better a navigator you become. Aidan and I both needed to force ourselves to be disciplined enough not to listen to the screams for speed, but to take it steadier, in particular to the first checkpoint, to enable our minds to become attuned to our surroundings and to make the relation-ship between this and those wonderful swirling contour lines on the map.

The following year we were back on the start line for the KIMM. This time we were in the Langholm Hills — a stretch of upland country almost slap bang on the Scotland-England border, about 30 miles north-east of Carlisle. Both of us had promised the other not to run when we started but to walk for the first ten minutes or so in order to collect our thoughts and ensure we were heading in the right direction. This worked. For the first time in three mountain marathons we found and dibbed the first checkpoint. We allowed ourselves to up our speed to a jog and so we continued around the course. It was a tough day — the Langholm Hills are not all that high but they are steep and there are a lot of them, the route planners had us climbing and descending seemingly all day. As we ran away from the final checkpoint towards the mid-way camp it was just beginning to get dark. Luckily for us we watched a procession of other B course runners descending from the final checkpoint with their head torches on from the relative comfort of our tent.

The following day passed fine — I did have to feed Aidan chocolate digestives in a bid to get him to run the last few miles but we finished without too many problems. It was a relief to finally complete a mountain marathon with Aidan.

Suckers for punishment, we entered the B class of the LAMM together the following summer. During the month before Aidan injured his ankle again and could not run, so I needed another teammate. By then most of my friends who would run the LAMM already were; I needed to find someone else. A quick look at the LAMM website, which had a page devoted to people seeking a partner to run with, showed that there was another woman hoping to find someone to run the B course with. I emailed her.

Kirsten was Scottish and lived in Stirling. She was after a new teammate as the friend she normally ran with was pregnant. We exchanged another email or two and agreed to run together. I don't think either of us was expecting to find another woman to run with (the vast majority of people who run mountain marathons are men) so it was a pleasant surprise.

As is usual for the LAMM, competitors only find out where the event is being held in the Highlands two days before the start of the race. On Thursday lunchtime we received news that it would be in Glen Carron, a great group of mountains in the north-west just south of Torridon.

I met up with Kirsten shortly after I arrived in Loch Carron on the Friday evening. She was really nice and very experienced at running, having done plenty of mountain marathons and then in the process of bagging all the Munros with her husband.

Despite being held on the closest weekend to mid-summer, the weather forecast was not at all good. We packed our heavier, more robust waterproofs and I packed extra cake.

I have never taken so much care getting to the first checkpoint! Running steady, sharing our thoughts on where it was, we soon found it. There was still a lot more to collect but at least we had dibbed that first one.

Throughout the day the weather got worse and worse. It was very windy with heavy rain that became sleet and then snow as we gained height on the mountains. At one point — at a high pass between two mountains — we became very cold, Kirsten more so than me. It got to a point where her hands would not function normally and we were both shivering uncontrollably. We had seen a number of teams retire during the day due to the conditions and were thinking that maybe we should do the same, although neither of us wanted to.

At this point we were about two thirds of the way around our course. We had a big climb to do to our final checkpoint for the day in the high bealach — pass — on the ridge between two of Glen Carron's Munros — Bidean an Eòin Deirg and Sgùrr a'Chaorachain. We figured this climb would warm us up. From this checkpoint, the quickest line to the finish was to follow the ridge as it curled northwards to the summit of Sgùrr a'Chaorachain, and then to descend off the nose of this mountain northwards. If we ran hard we would stay warm until we were down in the valley at the overnight campsite. We resolved to continue, and I (literally) fed Kirsten jelly babies — putting them in her mouth one at a time as she could not use her hands. We climbed the hill via a steep gully and ran like the clappers off of it, fortunately in the right direction. We arrived at the bog that was the day's finish and campsite and found as dry a place as possible on which to pitch the tent.

We stayed warm and dry in our little tent that night. The following morning dawned much calmer — blue skies and the sun contrasted with the previous day's gloom, displaying Glen Carron in an altogether different guise.

The second day passed much more comfortably. The only real worry we had was when we were descending a steep hillside and came across near vertical craggy ground that we needed to get through or otherwise take a lengthy detour. We found a line of least steepness, a small broken stream and little waterfall. Peering over the edge we still were not sure: it was not very high but we could not see if we could climb down safely. After a bit of joint prevarication, Kirsten threw her map down where we intended to climb, declaring that we now had to go that way otherwise we would lose her map. That made me smile. We climbed down, and carried on following our line into the glen.

We reached the finish with big smiles on our faces. With the hot sun shining on our faces the chills on the high ground the day before were a distant memory — we made the right decision not to retire from the race. It had been tough, but it felt great to have made it through to the finish, and with no navigational howlers to boot. This boosted my confidence and it had certainly helped running with someone as experienced in the hills as Kirsten. Maybe I was also finally starting to improve.

A few weeks after running in Glen Carron, I was out having drinks with friends from Otley, several of whom had also run in the event. We started to discuss the difficulty and length of the courses. One of us had run the Elite and was saying just how much tougher he thought it was compared to the A, B and C courses. I'd had a beer or two and declared that I could do the Elite, that I might not be able to do it immediately, but that I would build up to it and sometime soon complete an Elite course.

I was met with incredulous looks. Fair enough really — I had only just finished a substantially easier course at the LAMM. Perhaps it was the beer talking! This was the first time I started to talk about trying to do the Elite, before that the idea had been stuck within the confines of my own thoughts. In my mind I saw the Elite on a pedestal, at least in part due to the nature of the way I had first interpreted it — watching two whippets with tiny rucksacks speed past The Wolf and I as we struggled to work out and complete our first KIMM. Back then it had seemed impossible; now in the pub in Otley it felt more tangible but still some distance from my grasp. I knew I would have to up my game. I had to become fitter, a better navigator and more experienced if I was ever to get there.

To begin with I decided to enter the A course of the KIMM that year, held in the Brecon Beacons. Aidan's ankle had become a bit of a long term injury — he did not want to risk damaging it further by training for and running the 40 or so hilly off-road miles we would cover over the course of the event. I needed another partner.

Like the time I ran with Kirsten, I ended up meeting my race partner the evening before we raced together. I picked up Iona Roberts from Bristol Airport and drove us both to the start of the race on the edge of the hills near Merthyr Tydfil. Like Kirsten, Iona was another tough Scot, and she came from a background of racing triathlons internationally. Some years younger than me, she has a huge amount of talent and I think at the time was rather jaded with the professional race scene — races like the KIMM were a refreshing change for her.

I hadn't been to the Brecon Beacons since we went camping there when I was about ten — I have vague memories of climbing Pen y Fan in wellington boots. I had forgotten just how beautiful they are. I can become so absorbed in the mountains of the Lake District and Scotland that I forget the UK has other hills that, while contrasting in character, are just as rewarding to visit and move across.

Despite having only just met, Iona and I had a lot to talk about; we got on well. It was a step up for both of us to the A class and so we were a little nervous.

Saturday morning dawned calm but misty — very misty. This made me worried, as it meant I would have to rely on a compass to guide us through. The bearing I took with the map and compass from the start line to our first checkpoint was the first bearing I had taken in any kind of anger. Until that point I had relied to some degree on the translation of the contours on the map to the shapes made by the land, but mostly to the direction of paths, roads, walls, rivers and other land features that made placement on the map easy. This was fine for mountain bike orienteering, of which I had done a lot, as you don't leave the paths, trails or roads. But less than 20-percent of the orienteering you do in a mountain marathon uses any kind of path. The vast majority of running is on the open fell, often with only the shape formed by the hillside to act as any kind of guide. While this is useful it is not enough, particularly in cloud — a compass is the only thing that can be used to direct you. (I'll not mention GPS as they are banned in mountain marathons and orienteering, and even if they were allowed I would not use one.)

It was revelatory to find the first checkpoint using the guidance from the map and particularly the compass — given the thick mist we were unlikely to have got anywhere close without it. I suddenly realised that using a compass is relatively easy, and furthermore that it is objective. Unless you are in one of those very unusual places such as the Cuillin Ridge on Skye, where the rock has magnetic properties and the compass needle goes haywire, if you are consistent in the way you use a compass it will consistently point you the direction in which you wish to go.

The mist remained thick for most of the day. We traversed the high ground around the Black Mountain steadily finding our checkpoints until we reached the day's finish and the overnight campsite.

We were surprised to be leading the other female pair running the same course by ten minutes. Wendy Dodds and Sarah Rowell are two extremely experienced and accomplished mountain runners — we had not expected to be ahead of them. As Wendy reminded me at the overnight camp, given the difference in mine and her ages of at least 25 years, our expectation should have been the other way around, and it is a mark of our respect to their experience and abilities that it was not.

Our lead did not last long into the following day. A cock-up between our second and third checkpoints meant that Sarah and Wendy overhauled us and they kept their lead to the finish. While this was disappointing it didn't really bother me, and I don't think Iona was too concerned. Our goal had been to complete the A class, and we did it without too many problems. As I drove Iona back to Bristol Airport we resolved to run together again.

Iona was keen to run the LAMM the following summer, and it didn't take a huge amount of persuasion for her to agree to us entering the Elite course. In the run up to the event I did lots of long runs and bike rides; I even did a bit of orienteering in an attempt to improve my navigation skills. Iona was training and racing hard too, so much so the week before the LAMM she badly sprained her ankle during a race in Bristol. I needed another partner, and in the short time I had was not all that hopeful that I'd find someone else who was keen to try and do the Elite course with me. Fortunately the first person I called — the only person who I thought would have done it — said yes.

I had known Helen Jackson for quite a few years, and she lived just over the hill from me in Bingley. In her early twenties Helen represented Great Britain on the international mountain running circuit, and also had an offer from the British Cycling federation to become a member of their mountain bike squad. She backed away from both, preferring instead to travel the world with a group of very talented hill runners and mountain bikers that formed the Salomon Adventure Race Team. I have never really spoken to her about why she chose adventure racing over the separate disciplines. I do remember her saying that she much preferred racing in a team to solo events, and knowing her like I do, she is an individual who loves to ride and run when and where she likes, and for as long as she wants to. I think she would have found it very hard to conform to any kind of training plan that had been scientifically devised for her by a cycling federation coach.

It would have been good to run again with Iona, but in Helen, like Iona, I had a strong partner who I knew would keep going, and could do so for hours and hours. We were both looking forward to it, and became even more excited later in the week when we found out that the LAMM was on Mull.

One of the Inner Hebrides, Mull is a short boat ride across the Firth of Lorn from the town of Oban, that itself sits on the west coast of the Highlands. I had never been before, and Helen's only experience was childhood family holidays.

The race organisers had chartered a Caledonian MacBrayne ferry to take us to the island on Friday night. Instead of the cars that normally drive into its lower decks, hundreds of runners walked on, each of us carrying everything we would need for the weekend.

We camped for the night in the grounds of Torosay Castle, and in the morning were shuttled in a bus to the roadside on the edge of Ben More — the island's highest hill and only Munro — where our course started. The mist was down, forming what looked to be a solid impenetrable mass about halfway up the mountainside. It was another day for trusting the compass and following bearings, getting a further feel for our location by the gradient on which we ran and the shape of the hills that surrounded us.

I found it hard. Intense thinking and concentration was required at all times. The mist stayed down for most of the day and we took hours to complete the course. At one point we must have wandered around for about three quarters of an hour in the mist, knowing that the checkpoint we were trying to find was close by but not being able to find it exactly. It was frustrating — it wasn't fitness or speed we lacked, but the ability to find the checkpoints in the dense mist. It took us over eleven hours to reach the overnight camp. In a number of ways the LAMM is an easier proposition than the OMM. The summertime means both warmer weather and longer days — and there are no cut-off times for finishers imposed by darkness.

Despite the time we were out we were not all that tired — we had not been moving fast enough. I had a sore right Achilles that I hoped would recover a little overnight. We rehydrated our noodles, ate them, drank tea and then settled down for a relatively comfortable night in the tent.

The following morning was a bit clearer. Throughout the day the mist gradually lifted. We even got a view from our last checkpoint as we descended a ridgeline that took us most of the way back to the castle and the finish. And finish we did. My first Elite course completed (Helen had done a few before). The skies cleared and we finally got to see Ben More and Mull's other fine mountains as we sat in the sun on the deck of the ferry back to Oban.

My sore Achilles developed into tendonitis and I would not run for six weeks afterwards. I could almost put up with that, particularly as I could still cycle — in July of that year I rode the TransAlp mountain bike race with my brother. What mattered was that I had finished an Elite mountain marathon.

The next challenge would be the KIMM.

SEVEN

CALDERDALE

The mud, the wind
The lonely, dull green moor
What is there to love?

The gritstone boulders, hewn rough in their
exposed place
Old cobbled packhorse roads traversing the peat
High on the hillside the monument so stark,
spearing the skyline with its imposition
The siren call of the curlew as she flies away
from her brood
Bustling mill-towns lying deep in the valley

So much to love
AUGUST 2010

The Brunshaw Road runs west out of the Lancashire mill town of Burnley. From the centre of the town, it passes the Turf Moor football ground and then begins to climb, moving away from the urban towards the moorland that skirts the edge of this town to the north and west.

I know this road well; when we were younger we would spend summer weeks with my Great Aunt Betty. She had a house on the Brunshaw, as did her sister Sybil. In later years my gran also moved to Burnley, and lived in the house next door to Sybil.

Betty and Sybil have spent almost all of their lives living in Burnley. Their elder sister — my gran — moved around the country with my grandpa's teaching jobs, eventually settling for some years in Plymouth. This was where my mum spent her teenage years before she went to university, and I remember spending many school holidays in their big sprawling house, set on the edge of Plymouth, looking out over the city and across the River Tamar to Cornwall beyond.

The three sisters were all born in Burnley, and brought up surrounded by the bustling mills in which the majority of the town's industry was based. Some years after my grandpa died my gran moved back to be close to her sisters, and while we had always visited Betty and Sybil once a year in the summer holidays, our trips north became more frequent.

After starting university in Leeds and climbing on the grit crags of West Yorkshire area I began to recall memories of childhood visits. My memories were hazy at first, but the first time I walked up to the Cow and Calf rocks on Ilkley Moor to go rock climbing, I recalled sitting near the rocks wrapped up against the wind and rain in a cagoule, a tupperware tub at my side, filling it with windberries — fruits of the moor, the plants of which grow among the heather and moorland grass. I remembered the pie Betty made us later that day that more than justified the time we had spent staining our fingers purple as we strived to collect enough of these small berries for a good pudding.

Betty loves the moors, her enthusiasm for walking and spending time on them knows no bounds. Her love for Pendle Hill, the lonely rounded fell to the north-west of Burnley on the edge of the Forest of Bowland, cannot be understated. She is a proud Lancastrian and it probably still irks her that I ended up living on the other side of the Pennines. We'd take trips during the school holidays, to Skipton, Ilkley, Malham and Ingleton, and on returning home she would say that it had been 'a lovely day in the Dales', but never 'a lovely day in the *Yorkshire* Dales'.

While I enjoyed the trips out with Betty I generally thought of northern England as a dreary and depressing place. From the comfort of the car, driving north to Burnley from Bristol, gazing out of the window at a grey and wet Saddleworth Moor as we headed west over the M62, I remember remarking to my dad just how lonely, grim and unhappy it all looked.

Not far from their houses on the Brunshaw Road the town peters out and the land becomes moor. The first time I ran out to the moor was on an August evening. I was visiting my gran, having spent the day at university in Leeds, securing a place to study maths from the following October. I hadn't made the A-level grades I needed to study medicine at Liverpool, and, still unsure of what I wanted to do for a career (come to think of it, I still am), maths at Leeds seemed a good alternative: a maths degree would surely be useful and Leeds seemed an interesting city.

It was a lovely late summer day. Catching the train across from Leeds to Burnley, through Halifax, along Calderdale to Hebden Bridge, then skirting the moor and crossing the county border, I arrived at Manchester Road station and was met by my gran and Betty. After this short journey I knew I had made a good decision; Leeds was 200 miles from Bristol and my then home, but having my gran an hour's train ride away was kind of reassuring.

I was eighteen and had been running for nine months. When I was thirteen I had started smoking, and at fifteen began regularly drinking a lot. At seventeen I was smoking between ten and twenty fags a day and, on leaving school and going to sixth-form college, had stopped doing any form of physical activity aside walking to and from the bus stop. I was unhealthy, unfit and overweight. I resolved to do something about it. I stopped smoking and, as an incentive to help me quit, I started to run.

At first I ran less than half a mile around the block from my mum's house. I would finish gasping, my heart-rate sky high, it would take ages for it to return to its normal beat. I ran five times a week and each week I would increase the distance. A month or so after I had started I found myself running a couple of miles.

And so it began. I still drank beer but I stopped smoking and the day after my eighteenth birthday, about five months after I started running, I ran my first race, a local 10k around a large park in Bristol.

I was in no doubt that beginning to run had changed me. I was obviously fitter and healthier, but I was also relishing the time spent collecting my thoughts, clearing my head of unnecessary debris. Invariably I ran by myself, and felt comfortable in my own company. Looking back, these times were the first where I had spent any discernible moments alone outside in open spaces. I loved it.

That summer evening in August I wanted to run from my gran's house up to the windmills, a group of around twenty wind turbines a few miles out of Burnley and to the side of the Long Causeway, a high moorland road that runs over to Hebden Bridge from the hamlet of Cliviger. My gran was worried about me doing this. Despite my intended route being less than five miles and the weather that evening staid, she did not want me to run out onto the moor by myself. I suppose she felt responsible for me and, as she had no car or knowledge of exactly where I would be, would not be able to help me if I got into any trouble.

I found this frustrating and stifling. I was an adult, I could make my own decisions and I did not think this run overtly risky. I went anyway but felt uncomfortable that in doing so I was worrying Gran, which was not my intention. In the following years, when I visited her from university and went running on the moor, she would ask me not to go and yet seemed almost proud of where I had been when I got back from my run. Despite her protests, I think she knew I would go anyway, and I always told her exactly where I was going. A grandmother's natural inclination to protect against a headstrong grandchild's determination to do led to a need for us both to compromise.

I ran up the Brunshaw Road, heading east and gently climbing out of the town. After a mile I turned left off the main road and onto the trail that leads up to Hurstwood reservoir. Past the water and up some more; I could see the windmills and continued to run towards them.

I was surrounded by nothing; everything. The flowering purple heather coloured the land, contrasting the wispy green moorland grass. A pair of short-eared owls flew softly over my head. The tinkling sound of the water as I crossed a stream. It was amazing.

How could I ever think this place depressing?

As the sun sank lower in the sky over Pendle Hill I reached the top of my climb to the windmills. These big metal beasts, so unnatural in their setting and yet so striking. Each gave a soft, deep whirring sound as their turbines harnessed nature's power.

I felt like I was being consumed by the land, becoming a part of it. On that still evening there was a great peace, I felt soothed. I think that this was the first time I had ever thought about these things and enjoyed such a moment; it was the start of something. Perhaps this is why Calderdale feels so special to me. It's where it all began.

As a child I think I misinterpreted desolate as depressing. The beauty of Calderdale is rugged, pared down to the bone. It is simple and harsh, the windswept moorland is desolate but it is also an amazing place to be. It is a different kind of wild compared to the remote parts of the Scottish Highlands, but perhaps it is the contrast of moorland and mill town – within no distance of each other and yet a world away in feel and place – that enhances the extremes of both.

A little north of the windmills, follow a path for a mile or so and you will meet the old Gorple road from Worsthorne that climbs gently up and over to Widdop and the Packhorse Inn above Hardcastle Crags. The crags and boulders that sit above Gorple reservoir have their own stories to tell; following a sharp arête on a large boulder in the middle of the crag is Yorkshire hardman John Dunne's extreme rock-climb *Carmen Picasso*.

Head west towards Todmorden and the Bridestones crop up where the flatter moorland plateau reaches the steep-sided Calder valley.

The boulders that form this gritstone outcrop have been weathered into fascinating shapes and formations. Again popular with rock-climbers, these rocks — in particular the individual Bride Stone — are legendary. Believed a source of fertility, newly married couples would together touch the Bride Stone and go on to have children. The moor has so much character and so many features, so many stories to tell. It is not far to Wycoller, to Withens and Haworth: Bronte country. This wild expanse that forms a natural border between Lancashire and Yorkshire is encircled by market and mill towns, and has inspired many over the years.

The borders for this land are formed by Burnley and Colne on the west, Skipton to the north, Halifax to the east, and Bacup to the south. Central to this old kingdom is Heptonstall, a small village hanging to the side of the steep valley formed by Calden Water that runs off the moor into Hebden Bridge, where it meets the Calder. Today Hepton-stall is well-visited by tourists and walkers; a beautiful pennine village with a back bone of millstone grit clear to see in its foundations and architecture. Centuries ago Heptonstall was an important strategic citadel, the capital of the sixth-century kingdom of Elmet. Back then Elmet encompassed an area that roughly forms the county of West Yorkshire today. These moors on which I run are what's left of this old kingdom, untouched by conurbation and industry. These remains of Elmet inspired a combined piece of poetry and photography far greater than any of my ramblings.

First published in 1979 as *Remains of Elmet* and republished in 1994 as simply *Elmet*, this collection is a collaborative work between two gifted artists, Fay Godwin and Ted Hughes: Godwin's black and white photographs and Hughes' poetry inspired by these photographs. Together, these images and words pay homage to the harsh beauty and wildness of the moor, and to the gritty, warm reality of the mill towns that encircle it.

Godwin took up photography relatively late for one who had so much success and recognition of her craft. In her mid-thirties she found that she enjoyed taking photographs of her two young sons. Despite no formal training in photography, she did not let this get in the way of her drive to capture the landscape and other scenes. She is most widely known for her collections of black and white images of rural and wild Britain, and published a number of these to great acclaim. In later years Godwin was President of the Ramblers' Association, and made an important and influential contribution to the establishment of the Countryside and Rights of Way Act 2000, a parliamentary act which became better known as the Right to Roam. You can see and feel from Godwin's photographs just how much she loved the land. How great it is that part of her legacy enables others to legally do the same.

Godwin's photographs in *Elmet* capture the gritty, honest, monochromatic reality of the mill towns and surrounding moorland. Frequently of the area in, around and above Heptonstall, Hebden Bridge and Mytholmroyd, there are also pictures of Colne and Queensbury. Hughes grew up in Calderdale. Although he moved around, eventually settling in Devon, the valley stayed with him as is evident in his poetry. Hughes' contribution to *Elmet* is in response to Godwin's photographs, and his love for his childhood and adolescent places shines through.

Before I came upon *Elmet*, I had encountered Hughes' work in other places, at different times in my life. At primary school, his novel *The Iron Man* was read aloud to my class. At seven years old it had an affect on me, I can still remember the storyline today. Years passed. While at university, I would read one of his later collections *Tales from Ovid*: Hughes' interpretation of classic Greek mythology. I was very familiar with these myths and legends; I had read them avidly as I was growing up. This poetry took the tales I knew so well from children's storybooks and at the same time smoothed and roughened them. His gift makes the words flow like treacle; slowly and richly, with deliberation. The rough edge comes from Hughes bringing a reality to the myths

— contextualising them to a more adult form, removing the saccharine that seems requisite of most literature for children.

Someone once asked which of Hughes and Godwin were the luckiest, as in this collection each enhances the other's work tremendously. Taken apart, the images and words are beautiful; together they are powerfully so.

There are few roads on which you could drive a car through this section of the Pennines; it is quicker to drive around than across. There are however a multitude of paths and tracks that traverse the moor in all directions. The car's loss is the bicycle's gain; these trails are great to walk and run, but I find them at their best when I ride a bike along them.

There is something about Calderdale that makes winter my preferred time to cycle over its moors. I find odd comfort in the mud, damp trails and puddles. Occasional low winter sunlight enhances the ochre bracken, long dead since the summer, setting it off against the tempered greens and yellows of the tussocks and moorland grasses. In winter it feels like the place is resting; recovering and rejuvenating before the mighty growth and renewal of spring. This cold, granular, basic feel of the land contrasts with the warmth of my body as I grind my way up its steep climbs and ride through and across wintered trails. I say 'grind' as that is what I am invariably doing, on my singlespeed mountain bike.

With so many great trails to ride in Calderdale it seems churlish to discuss favourites, but one I always enjoy and which lingers in my memory climbs up from from Cragg Vale, a small village that sits on the Blackstone Edge road, a few miles south of Mytholmroyd. The track gently ascends to Withens Clough reservoir, set in Withens Moor on the back of Stoodley Pike, a prominent hill above Hebden Bridge, Todmorden and Mytholmroyd. Withens Clough sits south of Stoodley Pike, and from this position the hill does not seem too imposing.

Viewed from the north however the fell is striking, made even more so by the huge obelisk of a monument at its summit, dominating the horizon on the southern edge of the valley. A memorial to the war-dead, the monument can be seen from miles around, and is one of the lasting visible impressions of Calderdale taken with you when you reach and leave the valley.

From the reservoir, the trail climbs steeply and diagonally up the fell side. It does not visit the summit of Stoodley Pike but instead crosses the western shoulder of the fell. Along the way the trail changes in its make-up from a wide soft-ish mixture of grass, mud and rock to a narrower, more sinuous singletrack formed by large cobbles lying end-to-end.

Cobbled trails like this criss-cross Calderdale and the gritstone Pennines. Crossing wild open moor, they epitomise the area, pitched centuries ago to enable the thoroughfare of packhorses — and therefore trade — between villages and towns. These tracks are still going strong; their robustness holding up to many years of use and weathering. Perhaps the most amazing thing is that they have not been consumed by the peat bog they cross. Maybe some have? These days they may not see much passing trade but out on the moor these Pennine cobbles are used and enjoyed by countless walkers, horse riders and cyclists.

I head north along the trail and crest the highest point of the climb. The Calder valley lies before me, its grit and beauty evident as I gaze across this steep-sided cleft from Blackshaw Head on one side to Staups Moor on the other. Stoodley Pike monument sits over my right shoulder in my peripheral vision. I put it from my mind and focus on riding the descent. The cobbles add some spice to the downhill — ride fast and I'll skim over them, more of a buzz than the jolt that each cobble will give if I ride them slowly. But ride too fast and the pain of a likely fall will be reminder enough that I should have feathered my brakes a little more. Riding descents like this is not too hard but is always challenging. A classic to ride, at the same time the scenery surrounding me and the terrain under my wheels invokes the feel of the place and its history.

This cobbled track descends to meet the old London Road at Mankinholes. The road is not metalled for much of its way, and forms a bridleway that runs along the lower north-west flank of Stoodley Pike. There is a photograph in *Elmet* of the trail making this descent, surrounded by a moody moor and brooding sky. Perhaps Godwin chose the scene — entitled 'Above Lumbutts' — because for her it typified the nature of the old packhorse routes in the same way it does for me. While these cobbled roads are far from natural, they are hewn from the land and blend into it in a way that suggests they have always been there.

The moor is a wild place, it belongs to no one. Things of wonder happen on and around it all the time. I feel lucky that I can spend time wandering and exploring, feeling freer, realising and releasing parts of my self that too often remain hidden in our society of process and control. It has taken me a while to appreciate how important places like Calderdale are to me. Now I understand more, I don't think I will take them for granted again.

EIGHT

RUNNING

I push down with my hands on the front of my legs, just above the knee. In time with each step I take upwards, I push down on my leading leg. This push adds to the force exerted by my leg to propel me upwards. I don't know if it has ever been measured how much this climbing style helps a fell runner but, at this point in this race, I need as much help as I can get.

I started too fast—again. It feels like I have nothing left in my legs. I squeeze down an energy gel and am left with the sticky remnants of it on both hands. I am very thirsty but have no water with me; I will have to wait until the next stream crossing. If I feel this bad for the remaining nine miles of this race, they will seem like at least twenty. At the moment I would give anything for a second wind, anything.

I shouldn't be surprised I feel like this, the Helvellyn Triathlon is still in my legs; it was less than a week ago after all. My body feels heavy and weary and I am only on Wetherlam, the first hill. I really should not be here today; my fatigue is not doing my potential any favours, I won't meet my aim of finishing in under two and a half hours. But I can't seem to keep away from this race. There are no hiding places and no space for excuses. I have no puncture, broken bike or other piece of equipment to fail. I'm having a bad one and it is down to me alone.

Go on, drop out. It doesn't matter, it's only a run around a few hills.

The thought crosses my mind and I immediately dismiss it. I may be feeling terrible but nowhere near bad enough to retire from this race; to give up, to fail. If I did it today then surely it would be easier to give up the next time I feel like this. I could spiral into a much easier acceptance of quitting; suddenly I would lose my drive to keep going. The fear of this is more than enough for me to press on. Getting the best out of yourself should not feel easy, and I have felt worse than this.

What doesn't kill you makes you stronger — who was it that said that?

I look around me — are others feeling this bad? Maybe. We all have rather telling expressions on our faces. As we climb this hill together we are each in our own little worlds of pain and deep breathing. We are racing one another, but that's secondary at the moment — let's get to the top of this hill first. Even then, while there are rivalries and strong competition, in reality we are only racing ourselves. No one really cares; we're all here for the same reason.

Because fell running is simple. Honest and real.

I love this fell race. It was one of my first, and my first in the Lake District. Every year, on a Saturday morning in mid-September, the Three Shires fell race starts from Little Langdale. Thirteen miles long, a tough and scenic route up Wetherlam, Swirl How, steeply down to cross the Wrynose Pass, up Pike o' Blisco and then — making sure you take the correct line off Blisco – a short but steep final climb up Lingmoor.

At the start line outside the Three Shires Hotel, two hundred or so runners line up. There is something very down to earth about the start line of a fell race; some gentle teasing, a bit of taking the piss out of anyone taking things too seriously, self-deprecating humour at what we are all about to put ourselves through. The race organiser, Selwyn Wright, stands on a wall and shouts a few instructions. All relate to our safety, ensuring that in each of our bumbags we are carrying the minimalist kit required — a whistle, map and compass and full body waterproof cover. We generally make light of it but the fells can be a dangerous place, and these few things can make the difference between an individual staying relatively warm and safe and becoming hypothermic, lost and in danger.

Before I know it, Selwyn is shouting 'Go!', as he jumps off the wall and in among us we start running. Down the lane, across the river, along the track and onto the open fell.

Finally, my empty legs deliver me to the top of Wetherlam. The first climb is generally the longest as fell races are usually horseshoe shaped or simpler out-and-backs. Once the first major hill-top is gained, while there will still be some significant descents and further climbs, none of them will be as long as the first. As a horseshoe, the Three Shires race follows this rule of thumb and, now I am up the top of the first climb, I am very thankful for it.

There are a couple of race marshalls at the summit and they appear out of the mist as I get closer to them. I shout my race number to them, thank them for their efforts and the time they have given to support this race, and then turn to my right, along the rocky path that forms 'The Band' — the ridge that connects Wetherlam with Swirl How. On reaching the col between these two fells there is a short but steep, rocky climb to the summit of Swirl How.

Heading to the steep descent down to the Wrynose Pass, I run along the ridge descending off Swirl How, along the grassy runners' trod to the immediate north of the rocky crest formed by Great Carrs. For a second or two I stop looking down to my feet and my immediate route ahead. Across the valley, the mist that shrouds Blisco is clearing. This scene — Red Tarn, Blisco and behind them the central Lakeland fells, all in clear definition after the rain with lines of wispy cloud clinging to them — is enough to completely take my mind off of the way my body is feeling. I may feel like shit but my god that is beautiful.

Immediately after passing the Three Shires Stone at the road crossing of the Wrynose there is the chance to get a drink at a fast running stream. Using my hand as a cup, I quickly gulp down as much as I can, and eat a handful of jelly babies. The climb up Blisco is steadier than the ascent of Wetherlam. I should be running but instead I walk, striding out in an effort to go faster. I am hopeful that the water and the sugar of the sweets will soon kick in, perhaps then I will feel able to run up this hill.

The descent off Blisco to the next road crossing and the bottom of Lingmoor is notorious in that it is both tricky to find and keep to the vague trod of a path, and there is a continuous pull to the left, down into Great Langdale. Venture too far to the left and all that will happen is that you miss the pass, and will have to regain precious lost height to get back on route. I have run this descent on a number of occasions, mostly during this race. Having got it very right but also very wrong, today I get it about right: my line is good but I end up having to negotiate craggy rocks about halfway down after missing the slightly lower trod that avoids this slower ground.

I finally get my second wind going up Lingmoor. To be honest, the way I felt when I started this race, it is more like my first wind. In comparison to how I felt on Wetherlam it feels like a turbo boost. I get a couple of comments from people who passed me on the way up Blisco as I pass them in turn. I respond by telling them that my body has finally warmed up. And it has, it now feels like I could keep going for hours. But I'm looking forward to the hot pie that will be handed to me soon, after I reach the top of this hill and descend off it, straight back to the pub at Little Langdale and the finish.

What a way to spend a Saturday morning.

At the end of the race we will wash our scratched and muddy legs in a stream in a field next to the pub, and share our feelings and experiences of the last few hours with the person whom moments previously we were desperately trying to beat in a sprint finish. Maybe have a pint or a cup of tea. Then each of us will head off, until the next time.

For a few the next time will be the day after, at the Dalehead race in Borrowdale. For others it will be the Ian Hodgson mountain relay or the Langdale Horseshoe. For me it will be the Three Peaks Cyclo-Cross.

The early autumn is my favourite time in the English fell racing calendar. Classic races abound, the evenings may be drawing in but the fresher air that autumn brings, the quieter fells and glowing colours lend themselves well to running in both an athletic and aesthetic sense. The sheer enjoyment to be had in getting out in the hills at this time of year, celebrating the beauty of the season, eeking out the remnants of summer and mixing them with the coolness of an autumn day, is truly liberating.

Liberation is a rather meaningful word, and using it in this context implies there is something I wish to find a release from. What fuels my desire for this release? The necessary evils that most of us have to partake in, at the very least to provide a roof over our heads and the means by which to make an escape. It must be more than that, the pull I have to mountains is so great. Heading for the hills. If it is an escape, is it escapism? Dictionary.com defines this noun as: *'the avoidance of reality by absorption of the mind in entertainment or in an imaginative situation or activity.'*

Then what is reality? *'A real thing or fact.'*

And real? *'Being an actual thing; having objective existence; not imaginary.'*

So, it is not escapism: the fells are as real as any urban environment, perhaps more so as they will stand the test of our time. In spending time in the hills we are escaping the mundane perhaps, but escape and escapism are two different things.

For a few hours my focus is entirely spent on the hills. This focus does not have space to be concerned about pressing project deadlines, the fact that the front door really does need painting, or that my dad is ill again.

The meeting of today's project deadline is tomorrow's forgotten achievement; in the grand scheme of things it really doesn't matter. The front door is a long way from being rotten. My dad's health is a different story; but it is not in my gift to make it better and I can't — I won't — let it drag me down.

Everyday life has its challenges, some of which can be significant. Dwell on them too long and they can take over. It is important to take time and make the capacity to resist their pull. There are times to focus on the everyday and times to step back and reflect. For me, spending time in the mountains is a part of this reflection and resistance, and in that they make me stronger. This time helps me to put into context the relative importance of these challenges, and to cope with the distress caused by those that are the most important and least controllable.

When I am in the hills, away from urbanity and other such trappings, it is easy to imagine that this 'normality' does not exist. How could it? The contrast between the vastness of a mountain range and a high street shopping centre is huge, but both of these places are reality.

This thought first struck me almost fifteen years ago, as I was crossing the Vallée Blanche in the Mont Blanc Massif. I was climbing the Mont Blanc du Tacul — a satellite peak of Mont Blanc itself, and a classic beginner's snow plod — with Sarah and The Wolf. The Vallée Blanche is a snow-covered glacier popular with skiers in the winter months and the start point of many Alpine mountaineering routes. We had travelled up on the Aiguille du Midi téléphérique from Chamonix and were spending a few nights camping on the glacier while climbing a couple of beginner's Alpine climbs — the Tacul and the Cosmiques Arête. It was my first time in such a place and at such a height. Being surrounded by jagged peaks and sunlit snow was both daunting and exciting. At night, gazing upwards, I had never before seen so many stars. During our second night there was an electric storm over in Italy. We stuck our heads out of the tent and watched the golden fission of lightning that it seemed we were actually above, fascinated and thankful that the storm was nowhere near us.

The early morning start to climb the Tacul was tough, but the stunning sunrise as the Aiguilles Rouges were lit up in a rosy glow more than recompensed. I was surrounded by such wonder, for the first time in such a place and it almost overwhelmed me. Climbing with friends in beautiful and challenging environments more than makes you feel that you are living.

A month later, back home and preparing to head up to Leeds from my mum's house in Bristol for my second year of study, I was shopping in the local high street. This was a place I knew so well; I had grown up in the area. Walking past the drab 1970s-built shopping centre and probably on a bit of a come down after such an amazing trip to the Alps, I remember asking myself if it had all been a dream. How could two such contrasting places exist within my consciousness; how could they both be real to me?

Given that both places are real, and while it would be fair to say that I visit one in order to placate the fact that I spend most of my time in the other, it is not escapism. More removing myself to a preferred reality, one that enables me to think with more clarity and to understand more fully. In a short space of time it is possible to be in such contrasting environments. The difference between a night-time run up and down Simon's Seat in Upper Wharfedale, and travelling on a packed tube train from King's Cross is huge. To be in these two places within a night's sleep of each other.

An early March evening and the sky is clear. It had been a beautiful spring day which was reflected by the night. A race: twenty or so runners toe an imaginary line outside the Craven Arms pub in Appletreewick. Each of us has a torch strapped to our heads, and we will run the five or so miles up to the trig point that sits on the gritstone boulders at the top of the fell and then back down to the pub.

And we're off.

The circle of light from our headtorches encases each one of us. Despite the proximity of others, the darkness makes me feel alone, in my own world. The opaqueness of my exhaled breath in the torch light at times obscures my view. I push hard up the hill, enjoying the feeling of progression and the flow of fresh oxygen around my body. Returning down the fell I try to let go, to trust my feet to land well and to propel me downwards.

A crescent moon sits in the starry sky. This night feels too good to be true; a chill in the air is replacing the warmth of the day. To the west there is just a touch of daylight left on the horizon; the promise and anticipation of the lighter evenings to come as summer approaches fills me with excitement. More nights of running in the hills, evenings of bouldering on the grit and blasting around the singletrack of the Chevin on my bike.

As I reach the finish, gasping, steam from my body diffuses into the night. A quick change, putting on lots of warm clothes — I get very cold in the half hour after a run like this as my body cools down. Into the pub, a pint or two, a bowl of chips and good conversation until I head home.

The morning after and an early rise, onto my bike and into Leeds before much other traffic has stirred. The train is full of people who look like me, suited and smart, travelling to the big city for important meetings and other business.

On arrival at King's Cross, I move with the flow of people from the platform to the Underground. It's so mechanistic, like a computer: don't think just do. I squeeze myself into a tube train. The compartment is full, behind me too many people want to get on, a voice on the tannoy tells them to wait. I avert my eyes from the man who is closer to me now than my lover usually sleeps. I glance around, we are all doing the same thing. Is my face as empty as theirs seem to me?

Despite the discomfort, the strange loneliness in being surrounded by hundreds of other people in this place, the intense feeling of being trapped, I feel content. I know of another place, not too far from here, where I am free.

If I could stand it, I could live in London. In the City I could ply my trade, maybe earn a packet in risk modelling and analysis; the work and research I do in healthcare statistics and systems architecture are directly translatable to the world of finance. I must admit that I would find applying my skills and knowledge in this area fascinating. I would learn so much.

But I could not stand it. While my mind's eye of bankers as brash, arrogant and egotistical may be clichéd and not always hold true, there is a falseness to material wealth: how much do you really need? The City itself is big and sprawling, there are pockets of green but they are not enough. Culturally London is an amazing place; so many things to see and do. It is great to visit but also great to leave. Instead I inhabit a kind of halfway house, working in the middle of a city, trying to do something useful when applying mathematical theory, while having the hills always close enough to be able to get release.

What I do know is that I need to think, to be mentally challenged. I would get bored and frustrated if I did not have a place for this kind of liberty, perhaps I would go mad. In studying and thinking I am doing much the same as running on the fells: exploring, wandering, pushing myself and seeing things anew. So I need both kinds of mountains. Spending time in them enables me to be content with myself.

I find the longer I spend in the mountains the further I go into them. The demands proffered by remote places differ from those of the everyday. The adjustment from the behaviours expected in today's society to those more suited to wild places is a steady but definite change. Just having a wee outside on the ground in remote country is enough to disgust some people. Why is that? It's where we came from, and it's where we will return. Perhaps it's the subconscious awareness of this, and the unwillingness to accept it, that leads to feigned disgust. Regressing, digressing, devolving, 'going native', becoming feral. Terms used to insult or disparage. But there is no shame here; where and what is the shame in becoming more natural?

Running on the fells can seem contradictory, and racing even more so. During a fell race I often spend a substantial proportion of it staring at my feet and the immediate way ahead. Despite being surrounded by mountains I do not look to them, I do not appreciate them visually as much as I could or perhaps should. I remember during my Bob Graham round, when I had reached the halfway point of High Raise, a fell set on the edge and to the east of the main Langdale Pikes, almost slap-bang in the middle of the Lake District, I allowed myself to look behind and to think where I had gone, but not to look ahead. Behind me were the Langdales, the Scafells, Kirk Fell, Great Gable, Pillar, Dalehead and more. I had already gone a long way. Ahead of me was Fairfield, the Helvellyn range, Blencathra, Great Calva, Skiddaw — and I knew it.

I would not however look at these hills, scan my eyes along the horizon and think about climbing them because it was all too much. Despite the beauty of the mountains in the late afternoon sun I kept my eyes firmly on my feet. In doing so I protected my mind from thinking too much about what I was in the process of doing: running 65 miles around 42 Lakeland fells in less than 24 hours. If I had thought about it too much, particularly at the halfway point, already very tired but with the same to do again, then perhaps I would have stopped at Dunmail Raise.

But despite refusing to think about the fells, I always felt amongst them, almost at one with them as my body traversed the line of least resistance across these 42 mountain tops. Running in the hills — or at least moving as fast as I can; I walked much of the Bob Graham and walk up plenty of hills in fell races — is to me is not a contradiction but an enhancement. I may not always be looking at the mountains but my feeling of being at one with them is magnified by the focus I need to have to move swiftly across distance amongst them.

The mountains — and mathematics — are places where I can lose myself. I am escaping to environments that are in some ways more abstract, but places that are as real as anywhere else I find myself. We make a choice, a trade-off between where we want to be and where we actually are. Some people refuse to trade, others have to; it is a choice, and a sacrifice either way. Maybe the beauty and my appreciation of mountainous places and mathematical theory are enhanced for me by the yearning I have for them when I am not within them.

I also think that part of me needs the emotional and intellectual challenges posed within my everyday life. These challenges may be interspaced with futility and materialism but they are physical and exist; I would never progress if I spent all my time dwelling in theory.

If I had to choose, I think the physical and mental mountains would win. I do not think I could stand to lose my routes into them. In a world of challenge, change, inconsistency and doubt, wild landscape and mathematical proof are two of the only things that stay the same.

On the Keswick Moot Hall steps having just finished the Bob Graham Round in June 2008.
Photo: Aidan Smith

NINE

MOUNTAIN MARATHON 4

We still had a way to go and darkness was creeping up on us. It had been a long day, made all the longer by my mistakes. The checkpoint we were looking for was about to close, which meant we would be timed out of the event if we did not find it, and then the other checkpoints before the finish and mid-way camp.

I looked down at the ground; despite the bog surrounding us we were standing on a flat patch of grass that was big enough to pitch a tent. Glancing at the dusky outline of Becky, I figured she was thinking the same as me; it was a long way to any road and the campsite was some distance from us. The shelter of the small valley we were in would take the major force out of the wind and allow us a relatively comfortable night wild camping out on the fell. We were both tired and despondent; ready to accept failure. Despite running for over ten hours we still could not finish the first day of the Elite course.

It was 2005, and the KIMM was being held in the north-eastern Lake District. The race started close to the northern tip of Ullswater, on the fell side above Pooley Bridge. The event area encompassed the far eastern Lake District; we were to cross the long ridge of High Street, head into the tranquil Boredale valley, to checkpoints near Howtown on the edge of the lake. From there we would head north, via the head of

Patterdale, into Kentmere and then further east to the quiet and desolate Wet Sleddale and Shap Fells. The mid-way campsite was on the eastern edge of these hills.

Given its location in one of the most remote and least trodden areas of the Lake District, it was kind of perverse that the grey ribbon and roar of the M6 motorway would be within sight and sound of the campsite. This part of the Lake District is an area that people often speed past, bound for the more populous and busy central and northern fells. In my opinion they are missing out on a treat; the far eastern Lakes are one of its gems, frequented by visitors who are seeking the peace and quiet that can always be found in the Lake District but that sometimes needs to be sought after rather than assumed. These fells, that skirt the tranquil Haweswater, are home to another kind of discerning visitor; the only golden eagle resident in England. Until recently there was a breeding pair nesting in the valley. The female died in 2007 but the male bird can still be seen, often soaring in the thermals, displaying in an attempt to attract a new mate.

It would be fair to say that these fells would receive more collective human traffic over the course of the KIMM weekend than they had seen for years, perhaps ever. Hundreds of pairs of runners would traverse them, looking to locate those ever elusive checkpoints as quickly as possible, before bedding down for the night in their lightweight tents, eating rehydrated food, sleeping fitfully and then doing the same thing again the following day.

The weather was fairly typical for late October. At times the rain was heavy and the wind strong. The autumnal colours of the fells were occasionally enhanced by low light, as the sun sporadically broke through the cloud and the mist cleared to give a characteristic Lakeland view. Becky and I had an early start time, the earliest in fact. In recognition of the fact that the Elite category is a particularly hard undertaking for female and mixed teams, the race organisers grant them the first start times. We were grateful for this as it afforded us as much daylight as possible. We toed the line at 8 a.m., waiting for the start horn to blast and to be handed our maps.

Almost straight away I made an error; we went high, over the High Street ridge to descend into the second checkpoint rather than dropping east into a stream valley and climbing up to it from below. When we got there we saw our friends, John and Steve, who had started half an hour behind us. They would be moving faster than us but they should not have made up this much time already. Angry with myself — I should have seen the better route choice — we pressed on.

I had not been in the Boredale valley before. Separated from the main valley of Patterdale by the long lake of Ullswater, its isolation ensures that it is normally a quiet place. While today was different — a couple of thousand runners would be passing through — it was good to see a new part of the Lakes.

We were passed by Al and Ifor Powell. Al commented that it was a runner's course and he was right; the terrain was fast underfoot, perfect for fleet-footed fell runners. His observation reinforced a fact that everyone knew of the Powell brothers: they are at their best in bad weather and rough terrain, where their general toughness and very strong orienteering skills shine through. The course this year did not favour them. It was too fast and those faster runners, some of whom were relatively poor navigators, would both be able to see where they were going and have many paths to follow.

Leaving Boredale heading north, we descended into the pronounced stream valley formed by Hayeswater Gill. A number of course routes overlapped here as the race planners forced the use of a footbridge to cross a deep and craggy streambed. After that we continued to head north, skirting around Hartsop fell heading towards Kentmere.

As the day went on we slowed our pace, but we still had a way to go until the finish. I think in her mind Becky had decided we were not going to get there. While this was the most realistic of views given the distance we had to cover, I still wanted to keep trying.

As we dropped from the beacon at the top of Caudale Moor into Kentmere I tried to up the pace — I believed we could still do it as long as we made no more mistakes. Iona, my teammate from the previous year, and her running partner Gareth caught up and ran with us for a while, they were attempting the Elite course too. It was good to see them and to briefly share our experiences and thoughts of the day before they chose another line and left us.

Kentmere is a beautiful valley, typical Lakeland in character. I had last been there on my mountain bike; having carried it up to the Nan Bield pass from the northern Haweswater side, I had found the descent from the pass incredible — amazing scenery combined with a fantastic singletrack trail to leave great memories. We dropped into the valley and crossed the Nan Bield trail as we climbed up to the checkpoint that was hidden behind a large boulder on the eastern side of the valley. From there we continued eastwards, climbing up to regain the valley crest, this time close to the summit of Kentmere Pike.

We crossed Longsleddale at the Gatescarth Pass and headed into the Shap fells. These hills are more typical of Scotland or mid-Wales than they are of the Lake District; tussock, bog and a distinct lack of footpaths are in marked contrast to their well-trodden neighbours. This was more typical mountain marathon terrain, the kind of stuff that can feel very slow-going and despondence-inducing as it drains your speed, energy and — depending on your frame of mind — spirit.

By this time our spirits were well and truly zapped. Our already fatigued bodies moved slowly towards the next checkpoint. In the growing darkness we followed a fence line; there was an indeterminate path next to it that made running easier. As it became darker, navigation would also be made easier in this sparse terrain by using an obvious map feature such as this fence; in the fading light it acted as a guide. I planned to take a bearing from a fence corner that would take us to a small valley bottom, upstream of the next checkpoint. We would then only have to follow the stream to reach it.

On reaching the fence corner, we bore off to our left, leaving the comfort of the slight path and fence behind. We had about ten minutes before the checkpoint would close. This would mean that, even if we found it, we could no longer complete the day's course, we would be timed out of the event and disqualified.

Stopping briefly to put on our headtorches, I realised the futility of still trying to finish the course. After this checkpoint, we still had two more to find before the finish and the campsite. These would be still harder to find in darkness and the time we had to reach them before they closed was tight. There would be no room for error and we would need to be moving at a faster pace. It was here we decided to pitch the tent, cook our food and sleep. The following morning, as soon as it was light, we would walk off the fell to the A6 Kendal–Shap road and try to hitch a lift as close to the event centre as we could.

It was not that we had not tried but we had failed. I was disappointed with myself for making the navigation errors that had slowed us down. While I still believe we had the speed and stamina in our legs to complete the course successfully, all the physical fitness in the world is not enough if you do not head in the right direction. Many a top fell runner would ruefully agree with me in that statement — over the years individuals have made themselves notorious by throwing away a seemingly unassailable lead over the chasing field, giving the race away by heading off course in the wrong direction. Hindsight is a wonderful thing, and so is having the skills and experience to navigate capably.

I am reminded of a billboard poster from about 25 years ago, when the great US track and field athlete Carl Lewis was in his prime. The poster is a side-on photograph of him, in typical running track 'on your marks' position, while he looks directly into the camera, a raised eyebrow indicates his bemusement. His toned and honed machine of a body is entirely indicative of the strength and power that lie within it; he looks ready to literally explode into action. Then you see his feet; he is wearing six inch red stiletto heels, which both explains his look of bemusement and entirely implodes your belief that, when off the blocks, he will be able to fulfill his potential. A canny piece of advertising for Pirelli tyres, whose company slogan is *'Power is nothing without control.'*

Infamous in the history of the Isle of Jura fell race was when reigning British fell champion Rob Jebb ran the wrong way. At the time he was leading the race and was minutes ahead of his rivals when he ran the wrong way off Corra Bheinn, the last hill of the race. Instead of hitting the road on the eastern side of the island, for a four mile run into the finish and a win of one of the most classic of Scottish hill races, he headed off the summit in the opposite direction, ending up in the rough terrain of the west of the island, which is extremely rarely trodden. There is only one road on Jura and Jebb was nowhere near it. Needless to say, despite being the best runner on Jura that day, he lost his lead and the race. To his credit he recomposed his location and finished the race, way down the field but still receiving his finisher's T-shirt. In 2008 he returned, this time a few days prior to the race and spent some time reccying the route. Jebb won the race that year, minutes ahead of the great Ian Holmes, his great friend and Bingley AC team mate.

'To know success you have to know failure.' I tell myself this when in the middle of something tough and daunting. I don't do this to reconcile myself to failing, but to remember that, if you leave your comfort zones behind and really push yourself, there is a good chance you may not succeed. The phrase is attributed to Tom Watson, serial entrepreneur and the founder, in 1924, of IBM. He is also quoted as saying:

'You can be discouraged by failure or you can learn from it. So go ahead and make mistakes. Make all you can. Because, remember that's where you'll find success. On the far side.'

Was it arrogance or self-belief? It was well over a year since I had declared over those beers in the pub in Otley that I had it in me to complete the Elite course. At times it can be easy for other people to misinterpret and confuse my determination as arrogance.

While I suppose I worry that I will seem immodest and boastful, I still fundamentally adhere to maintaining a strong belief in success. I don't think it is necessary to always be voluble about this belief but, if someone asks me of my intentions I will tell them, and to them the intended outcome may seem unlikely. If you listen to their doubts, and then let your own creep in, that is tantamount to preparing yourself for failure.

Why did I believe I had it in me to complete an OMM Elite course? There are plenty of far better runners than me who would not even consider trying. I believed I had it in me because I wanted to do it. What I was attempting was not uncharted. Other women had done it before and I had completed the LAMM Elite course on Mull with Helen. I knew I would need to train and prepare myself properly, and that this preparation builds confidence. Building confidence is important but so too is boldness. I do not believe in accepting limits that have been set for me by other people. What do they know about what I can achieve? Of course there are limits; times when the objective is either impossible or when the opportunity has passed. These are the times to give in gracefully, to put your tent up on the fell and fall asleep.

Our night on the fell passed pretty comfortably, save for the few minutes when I thought I had not packed the matches and frantically searched for them. My desire to light our stove, brew up hot chocolate and noodles and not risk the wrath of Becky going hungry due to my forgetfulness was strong. I found them and we were soon all the warmer for hot food and drink. While we were both disappointed and deflated we were still laughing. Becky was bemused by my balloon bed and sleeping bag that only had insulation on the upper facing side — the wonders and comfort of lightweight kit and the sacrifices competitors make to ensure their rucksacks are as light as possible!

The OMM is only a race; a weekend spent in the hills with friends. Although failing to complete the event is frustrating, this failure is a long way away from the end of the world. We do these things in our leisure time, for fun, and that is the most important thing to remember. I love spending time running in the fells, physically challenged by the terrain and mentally by the map and its interpretation. The experience of this particular event would just help me to learn and make me more determined for the next time.

And there would be a next time.

In the morning we wandered down to the road and were lucky to hitch a lift with a woman whose brother was also racing the OMM. She gave us a lift all the way to the race HQ despite the fact it was a few miles out of her way. The weather had really closed in on the fell tops overnight; the second day's course had been shortened to reflect this deterioration and the fact that in general that year all of the courses, from the C to Elite, had been planned optimistically: they were slightly over-long. We checked in with the organisers so they knew we were safe and not still shivering on the hill.

The race planner, Debbie Thompson, was a friend of Becky's and a veteran herself of the OMM Elite category. She had had her own successes and failures at the Elite and empathised with our weekend's experiences. At the same time I complained about the fact that the checkpoints closed and timed out competitors; I thought it unfair for slower moving teams and felt that, unusual in the fact that we were a female team, we had been hard done by. We weren't the only teams timed out that weekend; some had even found every checkpoint and had therefore completed the full course, only to be disqualified afterwards.

In years of particularly bad weather it is not unusual for there to be a 50-percent drop out rate on the Elite, and it is never really a surprise when a female or mixed team fails to complete the Elite OMM. This course it set to test the fastest and best navigators, and these are, unsurprisingly, men. However, at times some of the strongest women hill runners have competed in the OMM, and over the years there have been some impressive results.

There is a verb that has developed over the last ten years amongst faster male mountain runners, in particular amongst Scottish hill runners. It is used most frequently immediately after a hill race:

'I was Mudged.'

To be 'Mudged' is to have been beaten by one of the best international hill runners of her generation, Angela Mudge. If Mudge runs a hill race she has not done before, more often than not she will break the record. If she has run the race before, it is reasonably likely she will break the record, and very likely that the previously established race record will be her own. In 2002, with her race partner Brendan Bolland in the Cheviot Hills, Mudge came very close to winning the Elite category of the OMM outright. The combination of Bolland's excellent navigation skills, his running speed and Mudge's ability to both stay with him and set the pace, meant that they were a very competitive team. The pair led the race overnight and eventually finished second in a tight race with Steve Birkinshaw and Morgan Donnelly, who overhauled their lead after a navigation error by the mixed pair.

Finishing behind Bolland and Mudge were some of the fastest male teams competing in mountain marathons, including the Powell brothers and Mark Hartell. Second place was a superb result, and serves as an example of what is possible for women in races such as the OMM. Of course, it helps if you happen to be an exceptionally talented hill runner like Mudge.

While I have nothing like the leg speed of Mudge — in a fell race I generally finish reasonably well but a fair way off the speed of the front women finishers, and a long way behind Mudge — I am stubborn. I will keep going and I will not give up. Over the years I have developed the stamina that enables me to do this physically, as well as mentally. In races like the OMM this stamina is as important as speed. I did believe that I had enough of both to enable me to finish the Elite category, which only added to my determination to do so. I never had any grand designs on doing as well as Mudge in the OMM, but I did feel I could finish respectably, mid-way through the field.

Of course, as I had been reminded again in the Lake District, speed and stamina is only half of the story; power is nothing without control. Navigation skills are something that need to be developed; worked on and learned over years. With map-reading and when choosing a route between A and B, over trackless terrain and under the pressure of time constraint such as in an event like the OMM, the runner is often confronted with myriad choices. The optimum solution — the most energy efficient — will not necessarily be obvious; options must be considered. Indecision wastes time, but the runner must give themselves time to think and make that decision. Once made, unless something goes fundamentally wrong, this decision should be stuck to; starting to go in one direction only to change to another slows you down.

More fundamental than my desire to complete an OMM Elite course, I wanted to be in a position where I could navigate myself on the hill in any situation. Any hill-goer knows that, when bad weather or darkness set in, the ability of the individual to reach their destination, to get themselves off the hill safely, marks them out as being properly competent in the hills. I wanted to be able to do this without the gadgets of a GPS or other electronic aid; a map and compass should be all I need. This self-reliance would afford me the freedom to set higher limits for myself, to head into wild and challenging places with an increased confidence and feeling of freedom.

TEN

MORNING RIDE

I cycle up the road that runs parallel to the airport. It is early. I have been on my bike for an hour or so and have watched the sun rise over the hill. It is a peaceful time, I feel calm and content, despite the fact that I am heading into work and will spend a large part of this fine day indoors in my office, away from the sun and the summer breeze.

On my right I hear the noise of an aeroplane approaching take-off speed. To my left another kind of bird is already in the air — a curlew gives its haunting cry as it strives to protect its nest by drawing my attention to itself, away from the ground.

Why do I feel so content? The view surrounding me is very familiar and this morning particularly beautiful. Wharfedale in the breaking sunlight, the air clean and freshened by overnight rain. This place and this view may be normal, but it is never mundane.

To the east, a wispy blanket of thin mist in the valley, the great inverted sinkhole of Almscliff crag and the viaduct are features in a tranquil, still-sleeping landscape. Out west, beyond the immediacy of Ilkley Moor, are the Dales and, further still, the Lakes. To the south the conurbations of Bradford, Halifax and other old industrial towns are bordered by rugged moor. Looking north, I know there are no major towns or cities until the urban sprawl of Glasgow and Edinburgh. I also know what lies between. Reassuringly open fell, wild remote places.

As I pedal, I wonder why I find these open places so reassuring. I find it enthralling that north beyond Otley, the town that forms my home in West Yorkshire, there are no significant other towns to speak of for hundreds of miles. Yes, there is Newcastle and Carlisle to the east and west, but direct? No suburbia, no shopping centres, no major development, nothing until you have travelled up the Pennines, crossed the border into the Southern Uplands and arrived on the edge of the towns of Lothian. On the way you would pass through or close to lonely and wondrous places such as Barden Moor, Swaledale, the Howgills, High Cup Nick and the border hills south of Tweeddale.

I need places like these. When I am not among them, sometimes it is enough just to know they exist. I can close my eyes and remember. At other times I yearn for them. I must visit to fill myself with a peace, a contentment that can bide me over until the next time — as long as it is not too long a wait.

In *A Book of Silence*, Sara Maitland recounts her own personal quest to find silence and explore its effects, and discusses the experiences and pleasures, and the trials and tribulations of others through history, as they deliberately sought silence, or encountered it along a journey of some kind. Maitland begins with the wilderness silence, and moves on to discuss the religious and other kinds of silence. Of course, silence is silence, and this is recognised in the book. A priest in search of redemption or some other kind of holiness is likely to travel into a wild place, so these two aspects can intertwine. On reading the book I felt that, while I am not a religious person, the spirituality proffered by open and remote places is a fundamental aspect of their importance to me.

Maitland discusses the fear of silence we seem to harbour in today's society. There is always some kind surrounding noise that removes it from us, indeed that we often actively strive to avoid it.

'Children disappear behind a wall of noise, their own TVs and computers in their own rooms; smoking carriages on trains have

morphed into 'quiet zones' but even the people sitting in them have music plugged into their ears. We all imagine that we want peace and quiet, that we value privacy and that the solitary and silent person is somehow more 'authentic' than the same person in a social crowd, but we seldom seek opportunities to enjoy it. We romanticise silence on the one hand and on the other feel that it is terrifying, dangerous to our mental health, a threat to our liberties and something to be avoided at all costs.'

One of Maitland's early retreats into silence was to spend 40 days alone in a croft in the shadow of Skye's Cuillin hills. She writes of how, during this time spent alone, her senses become more acute; that her taste and hearing are enhanced. Spending her time reading, meditating, writing and walking, Maitland recounts a sensation she experiences during a walk from the croft, as she sits on a boulder in a bealach that forms a watershed of Glen Brittle and Glen Sligachan, surrounded by the towering and magnificent Cuillin.

'I sat on a rock and ate a cheese sandwich — and thought I was perfectly happy. It was so huge. And so wild and so empty and so free. And there, quite suddenly and unexpectedly, I slipped a gear, or something like that. There was not me or the landscape, but a kind on oneness.'

Just over the hill from where Maitland sat on her rock, in the rugged, wonderfully isolated valley of Coruisk, Robert MacFarlane describes a perhaps similar experience in his book *The Wild Places*. With his friend Richard, MacFarlane had spent a few nights in the Coruisk Hut — a small bunkhouse on the edge of the mountains, where the valley's loch meets the sea. He discusses the feelings he has after swimming out to a small island in the loch early in the morning. He is lying on his back on the island, everything is calm and still

'After about three or four minutes, I found myself struck by a sensation of inverted vertigo, of being on the point of falling upwards. The air was empty of indicators of space or time, empty, too, of markers of depth.

There was no noise except the discreet lapping of water against the island. Lying there, with no human trace except the rim of my own eyes, I could feel a silence that reached backwards to the Ice Age.'

In each chapter of the book, MacFarlane visits a different wild place, each of which constitutes to him a different aspect of wilderness — an island, a mountain summit, a valley, a ridge. The first and last chapters tell of time spent in a beech wood close to his home, and so he turns full circle in his wanderings. Many of the places he visits are in the west and north of Scotland; I love his prose as he describes places known and important to me: Rannoch Moor, Buachaille Etive Mor, Glencoe's Lost Valley. Throughout the book he moves closer to his home in the south of England, as he starts with amazingly rugged and remote places like Ben Hope — the most northerly Munro — and Coruisk, before proceeding to what could be described as more tame, but which still had lost wild aspects he was exploring.

I recognised the moments, the experiences that both Maitland and MacFarlane describe on their visit to the Cuillin, as I have had similar moments of my own. They are amazing, fulfilling times, which are perhaps addictive in their intensity, as they serve to fill me with a complete sense of contentment and awareness.

Skye's Trotternish Ridge is an awe-inspiring place. On the north-east of the island, it begins to the north of the island's main town, Portree. Linking such amazing rock formations as The Storr — with its famous Old Man — and the Quiraing, the ridge is an inland granite cliff. On its eastern side is a cliff face and sheer drop, with a much shallower and gentle grassy descent to the west. Aidan and I were spending a week on Skye in September 2007, sea-kayaking, running, and had packed our climbing gear as we hoped to traverse the Cuillin ridge. The weather had not been friendly enough for this, the cloud hung low over the renowned black peaks for seemingly our whole visit. We turned our attention to the Trotternish; if Skye had no Cuillin it is this ridge that would be the crowd-puller, an amazing geographical formation, and a truly remote place, particularly as it is probably the less visited of these two ridges on the island. Starting on the edge of Portree in the early afternoon of a grey day, I planned to run along the 20 miles of the ridge, to meet Aidan at the Quiraing in the evening.

Sometimes I love running by myself. Alone with my thoughts and the hills, time passes. I suddenly find myself at my destination with no real recollection of progression. In the first five miles of my run along the Trotternish, I did not feel like this at all. I was lonely. It is often good to have company in the hills, I love the time I spend with Aidan in these places and I missed him. He was unwell and not up to the full run along the ridge so had decided not to come with me. I also felt tired and was quite aware that I still had another fifteen or so miles to go before I could stop. I thought of bailing but the only real way to go was back to Portree. As I was due to meet Aidan at the other end of the ridge, with no means of telling him otherwise, I reconciled myself to the fact that it would be easiest to keep going. I was feeling a bit sorry for myself.

I had stopped running and was walking along, trying to reach a decision. Just south of the summit of The Storr, I heard bird call in Coire Faoin, the basin formed by the steep cliffs of two ridges running off to the east of the main ridge, that I was standing above. Below me, two golden eagles, a parent and offspring, were gliding on thermals resulting from the wind and cliffs. Giving their familiar high pitched call, they swooped and played around; their huge span and wing tip feathers gave them an air of majesty — lord and lady of their environment, which of course they are.

To watch these huge birds from above was incredible, just the three of us in the remote and beautiful Trotternish. I had seen eagles before but always from a greater distance, and always fleetingly; this time I watched for what seemed like an age. My feelings of self-pity and loneliness vanished. I felt so lucky to be in such a place, feeling at one with my surroundings. When I finally said my farewells to the eagles and started running along the ridge again, it was with a renewed vigour, I was in a special place on a special day.

While MacFarlane writes of the Lake District with disdain in his book, saying that it is too populous, with too many paths to be truly remote, it is here where I have probably had my most vivid experience of this kind in the hills.

It was a Sunday in late January and I was spending the weekend going over about half of the Bob Graham round. I had started in Keswick on the Saturday and, having spent the night in Wasdale, I was heading over the Scafells and Langdale Pikes to Dunmail Raise. The weather was amazing, blue sky with no cloud, a cold wind but it was not too strong. The colours of the hills and valleys were enhanced by the low winter sun.

Over that weekend I saw so many superlative views of the fells that they almost blew my mind. I will never forget running off Yewbarrow into Wasdale as the sun set, giving Kirkfell, Great Gable and Scafell an incredible pinky-red glow. The clarity of the air was incredible. The following day, again during sunset, from the top of Steel Fell there was the same pinky-red glow, this time enhancing a perfect reflection of the round mountain of Skiddaw on Thirlmere.

But the moment that most took me was on Sunday morning, on the top of the day's first summit, Scafell. Always just a little further away than its slightly larger neighbour Scafell Pike, and separated by the tight ridge of Mickledore and the infamous rock scramble Broad Stand, Scafell does not see as much passing traffic as the Pike. I had climbed the fell up the grassy way from Wasdale, and I remember thinking to myself that one reason why my choice of doing the Bob

Graham anti-clockwise would be a good one is that it meant I left Wasdale up this steady climb, the clockwise alternative being the steep and rough ascent to Yewbarrow, which would take much out of already tired legs.

It was an amazing winter morning; sunny again, a cloudless sky and this time there was no wind. As I approached the summit, I had a look at the map to check the way off towards Scafell Pike, and ate a few sweets. The wrappers made a loud rustling noise that intruded on my thoughts. I stuffed them into my pocket. When I had stopped I realised something that completely startled me. I was alone on the second largest hill in England, surrounded by stunning vistas. And silence. Complete and utter silence. If I held my breath I could not hear a thing. I looked around with an amazing feeling of being at one with my surroundings; the sky, the rocky summit cairn, everything, everywhere. Much like Maitland describes of her time sat in the bealach on Skye, it was an immense feeling of oneness.

Reassurance is a feeling I have already alluded to, and it is a key aspect of why these experiences are so soothing. In the middle of such wild beauty, I am reminded of my insignificance. All my worries, burdens and issues don't matter in this wild place so should they matter to me? If this sounds like escapism maybe it is. Perhaps it also contextualises the important things in life.

When I head out to the hills I do not actively seek moments like these. I think if I did then I would frequently be disappointed. These moments creep up on you, they catch you unawares. Maybe it is no coincidence that Maitland and MacFarlane both tell of their feelings on the Cuillin; it is such a wonderful and unique place. But as Mac-Farlane seems to learn as he writes his book, sometimes you do not have to go too far from home.

Once, as I was cycling over Ilkley Moor on a particularly muddy

November day, I paused beside the trig point; the sky had turned red. It had happened in an instant, everywhere was lit with an intense colouring that spanned from Lower Wharfedale, up the valley, as far as I could see. The moment had caught me completely by surprise.

While I don't seek out these moments, they give me an immense pleasure when I find them — or they find me. Quiet beauty, in a wild, remote place. I can't get to these places all of the time, but I can get close; and the peace found in an early morning helps with this closeness.

My body feels awakened by the morning ride. Getting out of bed to ride, run or swim before the day really starts rarely feels a chore as I know it will serve to appease my needs for open space and thinking time. My mind is free to wander and my body is getting its required wake-up.

So, I am content.

Then suddenly — shockingly — I see your eyes. It is as if the tranquility found in my contentment has lowered my defences and left me exposed.

As the curlew calls and I grind away at the pedals, your eyes bore into me, reminding me that the memories and fear are always there. I can push them away, bury them deep inside, hide them with physical and mental challenge, and with the love and affection of friends. But they remain nonetheless.

The look on your face when you told me all those years ago. Your paranoid fantasies, all too real in your mind. They were all out to get you. The world revolved around you. You had the power to save the world and they knew; it's why they were watching you.

I knew then that you were wrong but could not understand why you were saying those things.

The fear that I will turn into you is a strong driver. Even now am I self-medicating, spinning these pedals? The beauty of the morning and the current flow of endorphins around my body are certainly therapeutic.

I sometimes worry what my state of mind would be like if I did not do these things. There is a fine line between training hard to reach your physical peak and overdoing it, succumbing to exhaustion, fatigue and illness. Is it the same with the mind and insanity?

Why am I so scared? Society rejects the mad — the insane. From the cruel jokes of children through to the bigoted opinion and judgement of those who presume to 'care'. I felt them all with you. How must you have felt? It was hard enough to laugh off the jokes of my school peers but my teachers and the church?

My teachers. Helping the young to learn is a big responsibility. I still cannot believe that some of those, during my earliest school years, allowed their bigoted judgements of an unwell man to impact on their judgement and abilities to impart knowledge objectively.

The church. That place had good people and bad. The good cared. It was sometimes misplaced but they cared. The rest, were they there so they could just feel good about themselves and better than others? I used to sit there, Sunday after Sunday, wondering why. Why people would sit there worshipping some entity, some myth?

Us humans, we have enough intelligence to understand evolution but some of us can't seem to handle its individual finite nature. Ultimately chaos governs everything. While we can control much of our lives, we cannot control it all. Things happen that we can do nothing about that impact our lives tremendously, sometimes for the good, at times for the bad. How can we handle this chaos? Should we put our faith in an entity that controls it? That everything that challenges us in life is controlled by the Lord, the Buddha, the Architect, the Programmer?

That's what these people were doing every Sunday and that's why those people presumed to judge you. Bigotry and hypocrisy based on fear and a need for control.

So madness then? We fear it because we do not fully understand it and therefore cannot control it. We try to control it. We used to use electricity — straight through the temples to numb the insanity.

Everything else got numbed along the way; people's characters were destroyed but — hey — they weren't mad anymore.

Reading *Zen and the Art of Motorcycle Maintenance* helped me to appreciate more things and to think differently, but perhaps most importantly, it helped me to realise that it wasn't wholly your fault. You didn't get electricity you got chemicals. You are now an addict. As our society tries to control something we don't yet understand we continually test new solutions on those whom we hope to make 'better'. Over the years you changed from an eloquent and thoughtful person, who could provide me with guidance and considered opinion to someone who requires constant looking after. You used to think; your classicist mind became obsessed with perfection. You started to think too much, you certainly worried too much. How hard must it have been for you to let go, to let me grow? Someone who was always falling off things and into things; I still am today.

I look at you and I cannot see that you are thinking. The chemicals that you are now so addicted to may control your mania but they have taken away so much more.

So, the roles have reversed, and many years before they normally do. I needed a life so I moved on. I still keep my distance while trying to reconcile my feelings of selfishness.

I think I am now realising that it is time to get closer. Time for me to grow some more, appreciate what I have and what you have given me. Strength, self-awareness, empathy — by-products and products of growing up with you. For all the challenging experiences I always knew you loved me. For a while I thought I hated you until my subconscious told me otherwise. What is there really to hate? There is a whole lot more to love.

The aeroplane takes off and the sound of the curlew grows distant. If I am self-medicating then so what? I live my life as I choose. I push my body and mind and sometimes wonder why I have such I desire to do so. Why can't I be happy sitting at home and watching TV?

The answer lies in the morning sunrise, the curlew calling, the euphoria of physical and mental achievement, the release of emotion and in so many other things, many of which I have yet to experience. As I push down on the pedals I am looking forward, to the next new thrill.

ELEVEN

MOUNTAIN MARATHON 5

On the evening of the first Friday in March, Edale village hall erupts into life. In the heart of the Peak District, Edale is famous for marking the beginning of the Pennine Way. It is here many a hillwalker has set off in good spirits, excited about the hundreds of miles ahead of them as they walk the length of the hills that form the spine of northern England.

On this particular Friday in March, the hall is full of people about to embark on a quite different challenge to the Pennine Way. While this challenge is far shorter than the long distance walk, it is in its own way tougher. The High Peak Marathon starts and finishes at Edale village hall.

A 42-mile mountain marathon, it follows the watershed of the Peak District's river Derwent, taking in the likes of Kinder Scout, Bleaklow, Lose Hill, Win Hill and Stanage Edge. It also traverses, for around 20 miles, the mainly trackless and featureless boggy ground that is the watershed between the boundary formed to the south and west by the A57 Sheffield-Manchester road.

This race is unique in that is a non-stop mountain marathon that is largely run in the hours of darkness. Teams of four start between 10 p.m. and midnight, and run the course through the night and into the following morning, visiting checkpoints along the way to prove that they have covered the full course. The winning teams generally take around nine hours and the slowest around sixteen. If there is snow on the ground or weather conditions are bad these times will be longer.

Given the nature of this race it may seem surprising that so many people want to do it that it is oversubscribed each year — the limit of 75 teams is always reached within days of entries opening. People are attracted by its challenge and its novelty — where else could you race in darkness for over 40 miles, almost entirely off-road and often over slow boggy ground with no discernable path?

When I heard about this race I could not wait to do it.

Looking back, during the three years following mine and Becky's aborted attempt to finish the OMM Elite category, it seemed I heeded the words of IBM's Tom Watson to the letter. I seemingly continually failed and thereafter strived to learn. In learning I practiced my navigation more, and in different ways. I went out running in unfamiliar hills in all kinds of weather, finding my way with only a map and compass in my hand. I entered orienteering events, and did many other races where reliance on my own navigational abilities was requisite for success — or otherwise.

The first orienteering race I did was on the Chevin, a place I thought I knew like the back of my hand. This feigned confidence — my assumed knowledge of place — did not do me many favours apart from serve me with a firm lesson of how wrong I can be. I ran around for what seemed like hours trying to find all of the checkpoints on my chosen course, which was only about three miles in length. I probably covered at least eight miles running around too fast for my navigational skills to cope with and frequently got 'lost' — losing my connection between the map and where I was on the ground.

This and other similar orienteering debacles helped me to realise a number of things specific to myself (I say this because I think different people have different methods) regarding the ways I interpret maps. Despite my familiarity or otherwise with the ground an orienteering course covers it is important to maintain objectivity, to focus on what the map is telling me and not what my own subjective memories or intuitions are suggesting. Maintaining the connection between place on the ground and place on the map is fundamental. If I run faster than I can do this, it all goes pear-shaped pretty quickly — the old orienteering adage of only run as fast as you can navigate is a wise one.

I got frustrated with the amount of mistakes I kept making. Orienteering is a navigation sport that relies on speed and quick thinking — the courses are relatively short with relatively short distances between checkpoints, much shorter than the distances between checkpoints in mountain marathons.

One of the key things in orienteering when presented with a choice of route is to make a decision and stick to it — changing your mind and direction while halfway to a checkpoint is a sure way to making slow progress and also increases the scope for making an error. I struggled to pick a line and stick to it, changing my mind in the belief I was making a mistake and in doing so certainly making a mistake. I wondered how those who raced around these courses so much faster than me could always pick the best line. Experience is one thing that would be very helpful, and many of these guys have been orienteering since they could walk. I had not.

It was very interesting to read a series of articles on the internet by top British orienteer Oli Johnson. They were really informative, giving a broad overview as well as hints and tips from an expert into what it takes to both start orienteering and to improve your orienteering skills. One of the main points he makes that sticks with me is that everyone — even the best orienteers — make mistakes. He writes that it is key to accept this, to recognise the key behaviours you frequently exhibit before making a mistake (so you can notice these behaviours and therefore catch the mistake before it is made), and to learn the best ways of handling mistakes when you do make them.

This was a revelation for me. Everyone makes mistakes: even the top guys. The key to coping with them is in their prediction and avoidance, or subsequent controlled handling — don't let the fact that you have made a mistake get to you.

In 2006 the OMM returned to Dumfries and Galloway, ten years after it had last been held in these hills and ten years since my first mountain marathon with The Wolf. It was my second go at the Elite course, and this time my partner in crime was Dave Wilby, a friend from Otley who I had done some adventure races with. With a typical fell runner's build — lanky and thin — Dave is a bit of a gentle giant; calm, modest and quiet in his approach to things, with an underlying steely determination.

The weather was not as bad as it had been a decade before, but a thick mist covered high ground for the entirety of the first day. We set off into the hills and found the first checkpoint without too much trouble. I found the second more tricky, the mist slowed my navigation down and the tussocks under our feet were hard going. About halfway through the day I made a mistake that lost us about an hour and a half. I was so frustrated with myself. The Elite course is too long to be able to get away with making errors of this scale. From then on we knew it was going to be very hard if not impossible to make the cut-offs towards the end of the day's route, like the year before we would get timed out. I had a feeling of despondency, a knowing that whatever we did now, however fast we could move, we would fail.

As daylight abated we came to a track we needed to cross to stay on course and in the race. From there we still had about three hours to go until we would reach the overnight campsite. This track was a way out, if we headed north-west along it for thirteen miles we would reach the marquees at the event centre. After some conversation we retired from the race. Dave looked as disappointed as I felt. We started to make our way back.

Dave and I were both disappointed about our failed attempt at the race but at the same time philosophical. To finish the Elite OMM we simply couldn't afford to make large navigational mistakes and I knew it. It felt like I was running up against a door that was shut firmly. I could keep running up hard against the door in an attempt to break it down or I could gently tease it open by working some more on my navigation and route finding skills. The latter would require a degree of patience I find hard, but I knew it would be more consistent in the longer term. Over the following years I bided my time and carried on practicing; as my abilities improved the door became less hard to open.

The following spring I ran the High Peak Marathon in a mixed team with three friends — Shane, Pete and Colin. As it crosses featureless boggy terrain at night, navigation is tricky, so Shane and Pete shared the role of navigator while I focused on keeping up with them and Colin.

The race has a staggered start, with teams begin running at two minute intervals from 10 p.m. until almost midnight; we started just after half past eleven. It is quite an experience to run through the night; whenever I do I always worry beforehand that I will feel a compelling urge to fall asleep at some inopportune moment. This hasn't happened yet, I just end up with a dazed feeling in the first hours of daylight and a thousand-yard stare whenever I do eventually reach the finish of whatever I am doing.

We completed the course in ten and a half hours, winning the mixed team category despite running around in a circle for a good quarter of an hour somewhere near Swains Head at about four in the morning.

This is a unique and perversely enjoyable race. I found a lot of satisfaction in completing it, and had a great time running with the three guys. We all shared a kind of laid-back but determined attitude that was conducive to enjoying ourselves along the way. I have to admit I would like to play a role in the navigation part of the race next time, and to run in an all-woman team. There will have to be a next time.

In June of the same year, Helen Jackson and I teamed up again for the LAMM. It was held in the far north-west of the Scottish Highlands, in the area of Sutherland called Assynt. I had heard of Assynt before — this is the land of the beautiful hills Stac Pollaidh, Suilven, Quinag, Arkle and many others — but even so I was not quite prepared for just how strikingly beautiful this place is. The hills, isolated from one another, rise up from their surroundings, each with its own individual presence over the land. Some of the oldest mountains in the world, the rock of these mountains is sandstone, and they were formed in and are the remnants of ancient riverbeds. Almost equidistant from each other — as if it was planned — the hills climb vertically and spikily out of the bog, striking features that give the area a unique feel and a unique beauty.

Helen and I were again racing the Elite course. On the first day this started near to Inchnadamph near Lochinver, and headed into the hills to the east of the Ullapool-Durness road. It was claggy, and I remember running along the ridge between the two mountains Ben More Assynt and Conival wishing for a view, which I imagined to be wonderful given the surrounding land and mountains to the west with the sea beyond.

The clag added to the challenge of the navigation but we had a pretty good first day, hitting the checkpoints fairly accurately. I was finally learning the fundamental importance of putting complete faith in the direction my compass tells me to go when I can't see for cloud, rain or darkness, and this was starting to make a difference.

After an amazing day of running in the hills we hit the last checkpoint dead-on and ran down the steep craggy descent to the overnight camp. This was in a remote location outside a bothy at Glencoul. With no road or track access, Martin Stone and his team of race organisers had travelled to it by boat from the road near Unapool.

We put the tent up in the early evening sun and I went to find Aidan who was running with Kate, one of our friends from Otley.

They had also had a good day, and looked to be as pleased as us to be camping in such a fine location for the evening. We had had a very satisfying day; it felt good to be able to complete the first day of an Elite course in a reasonably straightforward fashion. I looked forward to the next day with a renewed confidence. It was misplaced.

Early the next morning, after a good night's sleep, Helen and I packed up our tent and headed to the start line. Once we had started, we found our route for the second day would take us first north, after which we would wind our way in a prevailing southerly direction, returning to Inchnadamph and the finish.

We never even made it to the first checkpoint.

The event maps were double-sided; on one side the scale was 1:25000, on the other the scale was 1:50000. The larger scale map was provided as some of the checkpoints were placed in locations that were very 'technical' — meaning the ground had many features which made exactly locating the checkpoint particularly challenging. As we ran to the first checkpoint Helen looked at the larger scale map while I looked at the smaller scale version on the other side. We needed to run along the track east up the glen and then north, up a burn that would lead us into the checkpoint. My logic was sound but we were running up a different glen and burn to the one where the checkpoint was located.

We were making a 'parallel error' — a mistake where you confuse two similar sized topological shapes and features on a map. In confusion, probably confounded by the fact that we were each looking at different versions of the same map, we had run up a glen and burn — but the wrong glen and burn. These features ran parallel to our intended course.

It was almost two hours before we realised our mistake, during which time we spent a fair while on the shallow ridge above the burn wandering around in the clag, trying to work out why the ground did not fit the map. They almost did fit each other, which is worse than when there is obvious disparity because I wasted more time persuading myself we were in the right place.

When I finally worked out what was wrong that was that. Given the amount of time we had wasted, the amount of time it would take us to get back on track and the length of the day ahead of us we had no choice but to call it quits. I think Helen had an inkling of the problem earlier than me and had tried to tell me. Why didn't I listen? My steadfastness was misplaced. I had been too stubborn again.

Hindsight was already with us; if only I'd had a proper look at the map and a think before we charged off at the start line just a couple of hours before. A few minutes is nothing in the scheme of things, and stopping still for this length of time to have a good look at the map and plan the route ahead can turn those few minutes into a few saved hours, and moreover make the difference between success and failure. I had found this out the hard way again. When would I learn?

We turned and headed for Inchnadamph via a more or less direct route. It was still a fair way back, and it took us over three hours. Helen and I had plenty of time to reflect as we followed small tracks that took us through the layers of wispy mist that hung about, clinging to the hillside, to the many granite bands and lochans. Although I was pissed off with myself I still took time to marvel at the land: Assynt is a very special place. Given my stubbornness, Helen had good reason to be pissed off with me too. I think she was a little but she did not show it. She is very talented and experienced at racing in the mountains, and was philosophical about the fact that these things sometimes happen. When we got back to Inchnadamph we ate a good meal and found Aidan who had finished his course and was a little weary as Kate had made him work hard for it. We got in Helen's car and headed back down south, towards the buildings and cities of tomorrow's day job.

At work the following day there was more time to reflect. I exchanged emails with Shane, who I had raced the High Peak Marathon with earlier in the year. Shane had been in Assynt too, racing the Elite course with his friend Simon Richardson. They had retired after spending hours searching for a checkpoint during the first day without success. I think he was even more frustrated with himself than I was with my mistakes. Like me this was not the first time Shane had made errors that had cost him a finish. Like me, this was not the first time that Shane had thrown away a mountain marathon due to mistakes and a lack of experience. Between us the frustration we shared was more than enough to stoke some fiery determination: within three emails we had agreed to run the OMM together that autumn. We would run the Elite course and this time we would finish it.

On a Friday morning later that year, I had the familiar feelings of growing excitement and trepidation that I always get before a mountain marathon. I had felt it the very first time, before we travelled up to Dumfries and Galloway all those years ago, when I did not really have a clue what I was letting myself in for. The excitement is an obvious, natural and positive feeling — anticipation of the coming weekend of running in mountains and the feeling of liberation this brings. The trepidation is the other side of the same coin — running in mountains is hard. One of the pulls of the mountains for me is that they are wild: I cannot control them, and to move safely through them I need to be ready for what they can throw at me. The trepidation comes from knowing how hard it is to cope with some of the things they can throw at you. Would whatever came our way be harder to cope with than anything either of us had had to manage in the mountains before? That feeling of unknown is a big pull. It's a bit contrived to look for it in a mountain marathon but it is an attraction of these races nonetheless. It was Nietzsche who said *'whatever doesn't kill you makes you stronger.'*

Shane and I travelled up to the event location — the Lowther Hills in the Scottish Borders — on the Friday afternoon. A talented rock-climber and entrepreneur (although I think he would laugh off that last title), Shane knew about pushing boundaries. He had spent the last six months presiding over the closure of the business he'd been the force in creating.

From nothing he had built a company that at its largest employed 20 people. He is the same age as me and had little prior experience of business — he started the company in his early twenties and for over five years it was successful and grew. The mistakes he must have made along the way meant he would have learned continually — and the learning curve must have been so steep. If these mistakes were born from taking risks then there was of course a positive flip side to them: many of them paid off, the business was a success and it grew. However, one mistake was too big — he tried to expand and branch out too fast and the business failed.

I think Shane was most upset about the people this affected, and he did his very best to ensure they were treated as well as possible. At the time of the race he was in a philosophical frame of mind. I think he had to be in order not to lose it as he watched the business he had built up and had put so much of himself into go into receivership and eventually be bought out in name by another. I could tell that he was in that space of rest, stepping back, reflecting and recoiling before his next venture (whatever that may be). For him the weekend would be a means of focusing entirely on something else, something that — like me — he had a strong desire to succeed at.

After arriving at the event centre and registering we put up a tent, ate our final meal of the day (carbo-loading meant there had been many) and went to sleep. We were one of the first to toe the staggered start line the following morning. Given the time of year the weather was pretty benign — it was overcast and grey but there was not much wind and it wasn't raining. The clag was down on the hills, which we knew would make navigation more challenging, but we were determined to practice what we had learned over the years — not to run off like headless chickens and to maintain the connection between our position on the map and the ground at all times.

Despite being in the same county as my previous two visits to Dumfries and Galloway for the OMM, the Lowther Hills are different underfoot to The Merrick and the (fantastically named) Range of the Awful Hand. The hills we crossed that weekend were less tussocky and more runnable, the going underfoot more forgiving.

We made steady progress through the day — Shane tried to up the pace to begin with but I held back. After about five hours this began to pay off; as other teams tired, we passed them and clawed back a few more places in the field. The weather came in as we crossed over one of the highest hills in the area – the strange top of Wanlockhead with its weather station that looks like some futuristic moon town (even more so when wispy swirls of mist were blowing around it).

The Lowther Hills are typical of the Scottish Borders in style — steep-sided with rounded tops, making for great running. It was good to run in a stretch of hills I had so often passed when driving on the motorway towards Glasgow and beyond to the Highlands. Too many times I had looked out of my car window, suppressing the urge to go for a run as I made my way further north.

We reached the finish of the first day in high spirits — this was the first time either of us had finished the first day of the Elite OMM and it felt good! We both knew that this was only half of the story; it could all go wrong tomorrow if we weren't careful. The care required began with getting the tent up, eating, drinking and then sleeping. Conditions had got worse — it was raining heavily with high winds.

Once inside the tent it was warmer and we began to dry off. I was pleased to have finished in the light; many teams were still running off the hillside when darkness fell.

The weather got worse throughout the night, but our little tent withstood the wind. Others were not so fortunate and had had to contend with a cold, windy and wet night with useless and sopping tent fabric flapping around them.

By the morning it had cleared and we were treated to a fine sunrise as we stood on the start line. We were leading the mixed team category and spent the day playing cat and mouse with Lewis and Jane Grundy, the second placed mixed pair. Lewis is a fine navigator, and picked many good lines along the course. Although we generally moved slightly faster than them it was usual to catch them after they had snook ahead along a better route. We more or less stuck with them all day, until the last but one checkpoint; they chose a low route to the last checkpoint while we stayed high, climbing and then traversing the hillside. Our decision paid off — we gained ten minutes or so on Jane and Lewis, which we hung onto until the finish.

The finish!

A feeling of weary elation hit me as we reached the end of the course. I think Shane felt it too; we were both so pleased to have finally done it. It had taken me a good few years and so many mistakes but at last I could feel satisfied rather than frustrated. I knew this feeling of satisfaction would not last long — it never does. The next challenge would come along soon enough, but I was determined to enjoy this; I knew how hard it had been to achieve.

TWELVE

VENTOUX

We start early that morning from Bédoin, a small town on the northern edge of the southern Provençal plain. It is already a beautiful September day, the air cooling with the onset of autumn but still fragrant; its sweetness famous, one of the attractions of this region of France.

The road starts to climb, gently at first. On my left I can see the summit of the Ventoux. The strange spiked weather station that is both entirely out of place but now so characteristic of the mountain is clear to see, set against the perfection of the sunlit blue sky. It is a great time of day to cycle up the mountain; fresh legs — well fresher at least — and no baking hot sun to burn down on us as we approach the summit; its bare slopes afford no shelter, limestone boulders just reflect the heat back at you, making it even more intense.

I say 'fresher' as the Ventoux was our first climb of the day. We are however on day eight of a ten day cycle ride that takes in over one hundred Alpine cols, covering more than 1200 miles and climbing in excess of 40,000 metres — and while our legs are now used to the distance and the climbing they are anything but fresh.

In cycle racing the Ventoux ranks up there with the legendary Galibier, Tourmalet and Alpe d'Huez: monumental climbs famous for their beauty and infamous for their toughness. During races such as the Tour de France these climbs often perversely do not choose the winner but the losers, the riders who crack as they make their way up relentless steep and winding roads. Over the years the Ventoux has made its fair share of such selections.

There are a number of different ways to climb this mountain: roads wind their way up from the south-west, north-west and east. Sometimes a single stage of the Tour will climb it more than once. The most famous, and widely acknowledged to be toughest ascent route, is from Bédoin. Twenty-one kilometres in length, this climb begins steadily as you cycle alongside farmland and orchards of well-tended fruit trees that skirt the mountainside. The road gets steeper as you leave the fields behind and reach areas of forest and rhododendron. Unusually for a long climb in France, the road up the Ventoux is not graduated by hairpin bends; while the road itself is never intensely steep — at its steepest a gradient of eleven percent — the lack of bends makes it unrelenting, it seems to go on and on. After fifteen kilometres the road leaves the forest and passes a restaurant — the Chalet Reynard. It is after this that the climb reaches the featureless limestone moraine that is so synonymous with the mountain: a strange lunar landscape, with no trees or other vegetation to offer shelter from the sun and wind, both of which can get incredibly intense.

I am riding the Ventoux and other amazing climbs as part of the inaugural Cent Cols Challenge. The name itself is self-explanatory; to complete the challenge we will ride over one hundred Alpine road cols, covering all the distance in between on our bikes. Starting at Thonon-les-Bains, on the edge of Lake Geneva, we head south-east through the Chablais and Savoie Alps; Albertville, Briançon and Sisteron, to the Maritime Alps and Nice. On our return we cycle a little further west, taking in the amazing Verdon Gorge, Provence, the Drôme, Vercors and Chartreuse regions, finishing ten days after we start, in Annecy. The Cent Cols is the brain-child of the event organiser Phil Deeker, himself no stranger to long-distance cycling.

In July 2007 he rode over one hundred cols in the Pyrenees and then cycled through the Ardèche and Cévennes regions to the Alps, where he did the same. In 27 days he cycled 2800 miles over 317 cols.

Phil and his wife Clare had meticulously and thoughtfully planned the route of the Cent Cols, ensuring we would get to appreciate the beauty of the regions we cycled through as well as experience the challenges of cycling the cols and well over one hundred miles a day for ten days. 'We' are 35 cyclists; 34 from the UK and one — Ira Ryan — from Portland, Oregon. We have differing backgrounds but all of us share the same goal of finishing the ride. While the challenge was timed and the fastest would receive a nominal prize, it isn't really about racing. This event is tough enough to make its completion more than sufficient prize; we are all focused on our individual challenge, but not to the point of disregarding others. The camaraderie and support we share amongst us is amazing.

I leave the fields behind, the road becomes tree-lined. Interspaced between the trees are thick rhododendron, their dark green leaves and the tree canopy above and around me filters out much of the early morning sunlight. This section of road is particularly steep, it just keeps on coming.

Just over three weeks before the start of the Cent Cols I had crashed my bike while cycling on Harris in the Outer Hebrides. The bike itself had snapped in two and my body was battered, bruised and very painful. Consequently, for the Cent Cols I was riding a new bike; this time stronger titanium rather than carbon fibre. I was also finding that some things are easier to rebuild than others. While it was expensive to buy a new bike, it was entirely possible to do so quickly, as my need for replacement dictated. Although the new bike lacked the familiarity of the old, and I had yet to find my ideal riding position on it, the new bike did its job and it did that job well. I was finding it far harder to regain and rebuild my confidence.

On Harris, I had crashed on a switchback in the road while descending. Over the Cent Cols I would experience countless switchbacks, many of which would have far more serious consequences if I skidded off the road. At first during the Cent Cols I found descending mentally exhausting as well as physically challenging. During the first big descent of the first day's ride, off the Col de Joux Plane to Samoëns, I realised it would take a while for me to build my confidence when descending back up to where it had been before the crash. Perversely, my fear and my reticence to maintain speed when descending around hairpins made me less fluid in my actions, my braking harsher and less staid, which actually made it more likely that I would come off my bike. I would curse and criticise this vicious circle that both slowed me down and stopped me enjoying the feeling of liberation that previously accompanied me when descending on my road bike. I had always felt in control; this loss was a frustrating feeling, like one of the aspects of cycling I most enjoyed had just upped and left.

Over the Cent Cols I became increasingly more comfortable, the fluidity slowly returned and by the end I was almost back to where I had been before the crash on Harris. Descending over 40,000 metres in that ten-day period was an intense rehabilitation, but one I began to enjoy after the first few days.

I pass the Chalet Reynard, about halfway up the mountain now, closer to the summit. Sometimes it feels like a thousand thoughts pass through my head when I am riding my bike. Particularly while riding uphill, there is the time and space to mull things over, to reflect and consider.

The Ventoux is a real whaleback of a hill, it seems to rise up out of nowhere, lying isolated on the edge of the Provençal plane. In this it is an anomaly compared to all the other climbs I have done and will do over these ten days of riding — most of these will follow the line of least resistance to crest at the saddle point that forms the mountain pass.

This morning I will reach the top of this mountain, and this road does not feel like the easiest line. It kicks up, I get out of the saddle for a while, the cadence of my legs increases and I pull harder with my arms on the brake hoods, this change in riding position gives my body some respite from the otherwise monotonous grinding of the pedals.

Does that sound right? The 'monotonous grinding' sounds boring, dull. It is anything but. I find I can reach a state of contemplation and clarity in climbs such as this one that is calm, peaceful, serene even.

I have reached the tree line; the dark green vegetation ends, I am now at the limestone moraine.

In 1967 the cyclist Tom Simpson collapsed and died in this place as he strived to gain time on his rivals in the Tour de France. An Englishman, World Champion and winner of many of cycling's classic races such as Milan–San Remo, the Tour of Flanders and the Paris-Nice stage race, and who at the time was striving to add the Maillot Jaune to this impressive palmeres, Simpson was a truly talented cyclist who pushed his body beyond the possible and paid the price. As he collapsed from his bike to the ground, onlookers rushed to help. He was heard to say a few, now legendary, words: *'Put me back on my bike.'*

His autopsy revealed drugs — amphetamines and others. The obsession, drug abuse and baking slopes of the Ventoux killed Simpson; an athlete not a machine. There's a memorial close to the roadside where he fell. Set back from the road, surrounded by the white limestone rubble moonscape, it is a fitting tribute to a champion, and a reminder of our mortality and fallibility. Is glory worth such a price?

It seems that cycling as a sport will be forever tainted by doping. The sad excuse of the new, youthful professional cyclist is that because everyone else does it they have to do it too. Make money instead of a summit the objective and people will always innovate to get there first. The cynical innovators are generally always one step ahead of those who are trying by more honest means. At least the honest can look themselves in the eye.

I pass the Simpson memorial, I'm close to the summit now. How many cyclists have climbed this hill? In paying homage to its aesthetic and history I am just one of so very many.

The rhythmic pushing down on the pedals begins to feel hypnotic, it certainly feels robotic; is it me riding this thing or a machine? If I keep on pushing I will eventually get to the top.

Although I am only on my first climb of the day I already feel tired, no doubt because of the hundred or so miles I rode the day before and the days before that. I know that I will get to the top of this climb and those that follow it today over the next one hundred miles, but I will begin to really feel the fatigue later on. I have resigned myself to this, in some bizarre way I am almost looking forward to it.

Road cycling is a very romantic sport, with a deep and intense history. The emotions that can be stirred among both riders and followers of the sport reflects this intensity. 'He knows how to suffer' is a compliment paid to those riders who are able to ride through the pain found in cycling long distances, in harsh weather conditions, over inhospitable terrain. In recent years there has been a renaissance in the sport, and also in the discussion of this 'suffering'. What does this mean? Is it a romanticising of sheer fatigue or is it something more? It is a strange meditative state, the rhythmic pushing of pedals and the mind closing down to pain and fatigue because it is the best way to cope with it; attempt to transcend, away from the reality, for it will be over sometime soon. Because that is just it: this state is temporary; it will pass as the climb plateaus, as the rain eases, at the end of the ride.

The memories of this near-transcendence are always beautiful. The pain and misery coming from the body is forgotten, all that's remembered is the displacement from reality, set in a context of cycling through mountains. There is romance and beauty in this place, a perverse enjoyment of the suffering, the aesthetic.

Kant, perhaps the greatest metaphysical philosopher, believed there to be a distinction between natural and artistic beauty, that the former was more valuable. He wrote of the importance of beauty; of its perceptions and experience, and of how it was needed to fully enable reason. I tried to read Kant's *Critique of Pure Reason* and have to admit to have found it hard going. In his more approachable *A Very Short Introduction to Kant*, philosopher Roger Scruton translates a passage from Kant's complex treatise:

'Only a rational being can experience beauty; and, without the experience of beauty, the exercise of reason is incomplete. It is only in our experience of nature that we grasp the relation of our faculties to the world, and so both understand our limitations, and the possibility of transcending them. Momentarily we stand outside that point of view, not so as to have knowledge of a transcendent world, but so as to perceive the harmony that exists between our faculties and the objects in relation to which they are employed.'

Is it this harmony that we reach and that, in romanticising these moments, we yearn to return to; these sublime moments of complete objectivity?

I reach the summit of the Ventoux and pause to take in the view. I snap out of a monotonic daze and become more aware of my surroundings again. A 360-degree panorama of beautiful countryside surrounds this mountain, and looking at it feels all the more satisfying for having ridden up to the summit from the plain that is now some way below me. I do not stop for long; I still have a long way to ride today, over another eleven wonderful Alpine cols.

These climbs, they never seem to stop coming.

THIRTEEN

MOUNTAIN MARATHON 6

Our journey south was full of smiles. Shane dropped me in Otley before heading back to his home in Sheffield. I don't think Aidan was used to me returning from an OMM happy rather than ruing errors and vowing to return the next year. The following day at work, instead of critically pulling it apart, I could smile at my colleagues when they asked me how my weekend had been — it had been just fine.

Just fine. Is that enough? What is there to rage against? What is there to learn from?

I may sound ungrateful but I am trying to be honest; it generally feels to me that the anticipation of and the work towards an achievement is always more fulfilling than the achievement itself. If something is easy then it's nowhere near as satisfying as getting something else the hard way, but even something that is really hard when achieved becomes something less mystic, more solid, something that exists and, while still very hard, it is something that can be achieved again.

I have solved the problem.

Was this a typical anticlimax? It did not take me long to focus on the next challenge.

2008, the year after the OMM in the Lowther Hills, was my 'best' for sporting achievements. Amongst other things, I completed the

Bob Graham Round in June. In July I won the week-long Mountain-X Alpine adventure race, and at the end of September I finally won the Three Peaks Cyclo-Cross.

To fell runners and many other mountain goers the Bob Graham Round will need no introduction. It is the 65 mile circumnavigation of the Lake District, covering 42 peaks, starting and finishing at the Moot Hall in the centre of Keswick. To say you have done the Bob Graham a runner must complete the course in under 24 hours — the record first set by Bob Graham in 1932. I did it anti-clockwise and completely buried myself and my shredded feet during the final descent off Skiddaw in the early hours. My time? 21 hours and 56 minutes.

The Mountain-X is the most incredible race. Held in the Haute Savoie region, over the course of six days the route effectively traverses the side of Mont Blanc and incorporates many disciplines — running, biking, white-water canoeing, rock climbing, canyoning, high-level mountaineering and via ferrata, all with an element of navigation underpinning them.

Every day we would race a different discipline hard and fast, and this would be followed by a shorter tough fell race each evening. I raced in a women's team with two amazing athletes, Anna Frost and Chez Frost, and we won the female category, placing respectably overall.

Chez, Anna and me just before the start of the mountaineering leg of the Mountain-X race in July 2008. *Photo: Dave Allaker*

Looking back I remember this week as really tough but the main thing that stands out is how lucky I was to be racing with two great and determined people, doing some of the most amazing things across some of the most beautiful terrain in the world.

The Three Peaks Cyclo-Cross — or 'Peaks — is the most amazing and crazy race; my favourite. It climbs the three Yorkshire Dales peaks of Ingleborough, Whernside and Pen-y-ghent and is always held on the last Sunday in September. Amazing for many reasons, probably the most important to me are that it covers both beautiful and tough ground. It is crazy because racers cover the 40-mile route on cyclo-cross bikes.

A 'cross bike looks like a road bike with drop handlebars and skinny tyres but has knobbly tyres and just slightly more powerful brakes. Cyclo-cross racing is normally akin to cross-country racing on foot — around parks and heathland on a Saturday or Sunday morning. The 'Peaks is nothing like this, roughly half and half off-road and road. When off-road the route is like a tough fell race; the bike-shouldering section up Simon Fell on the way up the first peak Ingleborough is like nothing else, unrelenting and intimidating to first timers and experienced racers alike, it is a rude-awakening as the lactic acid already starts burning in your calves less than five miles into the race.

The 'Peaks was one of those races I knew I had to do as soon as I learned of its existence. The year was 1999, and I was 22. I got around in something over five hours and was hooked, coming back year after year and getting faster each time. It is probably the race I most wanted to win — I was second and third so many times I lost count. In 2008 I decided to give it the best shot I could.

The end of September came around and I was feeling strong, still rebounding off the intensity of the Mountain-X. This race had worn me out, but — along with the Bob Graham — it had laid the foundations for my best stretch of fitness ever. In the months after the Mountain-X I complemented this base fitness by training sensibly (for a change) — good quality interval sessions were interspaced between steady recovery runs and bike rides. I lost weight, which was particularly helpful during the 'Peaks; running up steep hills with a bike on my shoulder — something you do for a fair few miles of the race route — is made easier when carrying a few less kilos in bodyweight.

And I did it — I finally won at my seventh attempt, in a time of three hours and fifty minutes, almost a quarter of an hour better than my previous fastest time.

Each of these three achievements felt fantastic, pushed me different ways and each took place in stunning mountain environments. I will never forget the colour of the central Lakeland fells — a pinkish hue — as I looked to them from Dalehead as the sun rose at four in the morning, or the feeling of remoteness both within and outside my body as I struggled to cope with the altitude as we approached our high point on the Aiguille de Glaciers; and the excitement tinged with nervousness as I descended Pen-y-ghent, knowing all I had to do was ride fast but with care to make the finish and finally win.

After the 'Peaks came October, the month of the OMM. I had figured the next natural challenge for it was to run the Elite in a female pair. It was great to run with Shane but, as he did the lion's share of the navigation over the weekend, all I really had to do was to focus on my running. For me that is not the full challenge of a mountain marathon. As well as the running I wanted to contribute fully to the navigation aspect of the OMM.

In addition to trying again to win the 'Peaks, another incentive I had for maintaining and building the fitness I had gained during the Mountain-X was that I had entered the OMM with Janet McIver. I did not know Janet all that well but I knew enough to want to improve my running to run with her, and even then she would still have to slow her natural pace considerably to run with me. Modest and unassuming, Janet was British fell running champion that year.

Her usual mountain marathon partner was injured and we had agreed earlier in the summer to run together in the OMM. I was a little afraid. Not of Janet and her temperament — she's a kind and thoughtful person — but I did not want to let her down. To run long distances in the mountains so fast, she must train very hard and look after herself. She also has an innate talent to which I would never come close. This worry proved a strong driver, and when the time came I had never been running better.

Sadly the OMM did not happen for either of us that year. Janet injured her knee during the Langdale Horseshoe fell race in early October and did not recover in time. With hindsight (and well after Janet has recovered) it was a good thing I did not race that weekend. Instead I spent the time frantically finishing off my MSc dissertation that was already late; I was up against the wire if I was to get it marked in time to graduate that year. For once I did not try and find a race partner in place of Janet but stayed home and wrote my thesis. In the end the OMM did not fully happen for anyone that year — it was cancelled at the end of day one due to the tremendously bad weather that hit the Lake District that weekend. It would have been good to be there and experience the extremes of the event but it was a good thing I was not, as it meant I finally got my MSc.

Almost a year later I got my arse well and truly kicked during the Ian Hodgson fell relay. This relay is a fantastic race that takes place each year on the first Sunday in October, and runs around a sort of elongated horseshoe in upper Patterdale in the Lake District. Starting from Brotherswater, the relay has four legs, and fell-running clubs from all over the country enter teams of eight runners, who run in pairs over each leg. Ilkley Harriers — my running club of the time — often contends for the female team win and this year it was no different — we had a slim lead over the Sheffield-based Dark Peak fell runners going into the final and toughest leg. I did not know that I was due to run this leg until I arrived at the start on the morning of the race.

Thanks to losing my mobile phone earlier in the week I had not found out that team plans had changed, instead of running the first leg I would be running the last with Andrea Priestley.

Andrea was far and away the fastest runner we had on our team. Seven years earlier she had been British fell running champion and, while at the time of the Ian Hodgson she raced far less, she maintained a prodigious running strength, in particular when running uphill. She had previously lived in Ilkley, but now lived right at the bottom of the Ochils near Stirling, and ran straight up the Dumyat before breakfast. Everyone was pretty scared of her, and certainly of running with her, as you knew you would be in for a pasting. It was not that Andrea meant to do this, but in a relay leg pair from a team trying to win the race, the weaker person is likely to be in a world of pain as they try their very best to tread the delicate balance of going as fast as they can while ensuring that they don't blow up altogether. When I arrived at the race that morning, in the space of about ten seconds I went from being the person likely to be the stronger over their leg to the person who would most definitely be the weakest, when I was told the plans had changed and that I was to run with Andrea.

I was tired from racing the 'Peaks the week before, and still had not regained my running legs after finishing the Cent Cols Challenge only three days before the 'Peaks. Cycling long distances tightens my hamstrings, decreases my leg stride and those long slow miles in the Alps did nothing for my speed. I had plenty of stamina but I did not need that today — I would be running for less than two hours. Yet, before I could make any excuses the race had started and I was still running the last leg with Andrea. I knew it was going to hurt.

Our leg started from a cricket field on the edge of Patterdale village, headed up St Sunday Crags along Hartsop above Howe, along the top for a while before steeply dropping off the ridge back down to Brotherswater and the finish. I hadn't run it before but Andrea knew the course well. All I had to do was follow her.

Our third leg runners had a great run, picking up a place to hand over to us leading the race. My heart sank as they ran into the field as they had tried so hard and it meant even more to the team to try and keep this place. We started a couple of minutes ahead of our perennial rivals, the ladies of the Sheffield-based Dark Peak fell runners.

Ironically enough Janet McIver and Karen Davison, her usual OMM running partner, came skipping past us towards the top of St Sunday Crag. I knew this would happen, and waiting for it felt like some sort of horrible purgatory. I ran up the hill as fast as I could knowing it was not fast enough to hold off Janet and Karen, the strongest runners of Dark Peak. I tried so hard — at the least I wanted to keep second place for the team — the ladies of Ambleside AC were not that far behind us and I wanted to hold them off. There were no hiding places, I was racing not just for myself but for a team and I tried my very hardest not to let them down.

On the other side of the coin, it was a walk in the park for Andrea. She was all smiles and full of encouragement as I reached the top of St Sunday Crags. As I followed her, everything external to me — other than where Andrea was — was a blur; I had no concept of which direction we were headed in, of where we would go next, I was just focused on following her and trying as hard as I could.

As always with these things, the pain did not last forever. It was a relief after a steep descent off Hart Crag to reach the finish at Brotherswater still in second place. Although it was kind of inevitable that it would happen, it felt bad to lose first. I would have really felt like I had let the team down if the Ambleside women had caught us too. I think the rest of the team knew I had tried my best; they certainly knew that me keeping Janet and Karen off with only a two-minute lead was always going to be a tall order, as even if I was on my very best form they would both be a lot faster than me.

Despite the painful experience, far from never wanting to run with Andrea again, we agreed immediately after the race that we would enter the OMM together. It was three weeks until the event, which that year was being held in the Elan Valley in mid-Wales — a beautiful and little-trodden part of the UK. She had done a couple of mountain marathons with her husband Mark years before, and had plenty of experience running around the Highlands in all weathers, so she knew what to expect. I was looking forward to running the OMM with Andrea. I knew I would have to temper my desire to run too fast after her — only run as fast as you can navigate — but it was great to have such a strong partner who was so keen to do the event.

The weekend soon came around and we travelled down to the event centre at Builth Wells on the Friday afternoon. We were again one of the first teams to start on Saturday morning, and off we went running into the hills to the first checkpoint. The going underfoot was often tussocky — the small rounded mounds of grass surrounded by bog made for slow going. The weather was kind — cloudy but clear enough — and we steadily made our way around the course. I kept to my own pace but it helped that Andrea moved faster — she helped me to get the best out of myself as I pushed a little harder to keep up.

Almost before I knew it we arrived at the overnight camp. We passed the evening chatting and laughing a lot. Andrea has a good sense of humour and we have quite a few shared interests (apart from running up mountains). In addition to working as a part-time social worker and university tutor, she was, like me, doing a part-time PhD. At the time we were both in similar places with our research: knowing the paths we wanted to follow, but finding their explanation difficult to convey to our supervisors. We were both finding this frustrating and it was good to talk it through with someone who understood. The conversation passed the time well, and soon it was time to sleep.

Sunday dawned a little brighter than the day before and we again steadily worked our way around the course. While I made a few slight errors with my navigation, these were soon corrected and I made no howlers. I found this quite surprising and very satisfying — perhaps

I was finally learning. The ground we traversed that day was less tussocky than the previous day's course, which made for faster running. We were running around the side of Drygarn Fawr, a beautiful hill riddled with interesting natural features of which course planners are so fond — so many places to put checkpoints that will be challenging to find. I stayed focused on the map throughout the day, interpreting its contours to the shape of the ground around me and keeping my place on both.

The sun shone as we ran down the final hill to the finish and that was that. While we were the only female pair running the Elite course that year we had a faster time around the course than all of the mixed teams, and finished about mid-way through the field. I was pleased and so was Andrea. I was also pleased that we made it around without any real mishaps; while the course was long with some tricky route choices it was doable — I felt I had come a long way over the previous few years.

I would never say that I have 'cracked' the Elite OMM. At the time of writing I have done it three times and, while this is three in a row, the next time I go back bad weather, bad navigation or some other lack of preparedness could quite easily end this run. It's a tough event that is very testing and does not relent easily. Whereas before I could not understand why the organisers seemed to revel in its toughness I think I do now. Sometimes far less than half the field will finish and they mean for it to be that way.

I do harbour a quiet satisfaction in the improvements that I have made over the years that have enabled me to run with and to achieve with friends who share the same ambitions. It took me perhaps four years after that slightly drunken claim in a pub in Otley that *I could do the Elite* to finally doing it. I don't think those I was drinking with believed me — it was quite a claim for someone who was struggling to navigate and complete a B course.

And while my navigation skills have improved there is still loads of room for more improvement. I still make howlers and I am sure I always will do, although hopefully their frequency will continue to decrease. Despite having done so many over the years, I still love doing mountain marathons. It's continuous problem solving under pressure. Thought-provoking and physically challenging, and all surrounded by places I love, spending time with people who share my love for the mountains and drive for pushing ourselves.

Nowadays the mountains almost rise up out of the map when I look at it — a much different interpretation to the strange flat swirls and loops I saw on that first KIMM back in 1996. There is something I find amazingly satisfying in looking at a map and translating it — understanding my place on the given terrain I am traversing. I get lost in the map and place. I don't mean that I don't know where I am, but that I find release and feel a part of the landscape. I can see it both with my eyes and with my mind and become absorbed — lost — in this thinking space. Alongside this, my body takes me to the places as instructed by my mind — they are at one, physically and mentally solving the same problem.

Winning the Three Peaks Cyclo-Cross, September 2008.
Photo: Aidan Smith

PART 3

TOUR DIVIDE

Upper Eskdale

FOURTEEN

PERFECTION

'Hell no! Me, riding the Tour Divide, do I look that crazy?'

He took off his sunglasses and stared at me; the tan lines on his face made by his glasses and helmet straps told me he had been riding his bike for a fair few days. Strapped to the back of his bike were two pannier bags and a rather large looking stuff sack that I assumed contained a tent.

We were standing outside a trading post in Swan Lake, Montana, the back end of nowhere, in the middle of a vast and beautiful mountain country; a long way from home. He looked as tired as I still felt; it was early evening and he had probably been cycling all day.

'Can I camp here?'

His next question. The trading post was closed, so he could no longer inquire with the owners, who also ran the campground and cabins in the wooded area out the back of their store and fuel-stop. I told him that I thought he could, and that the owners lived in the house set away from the cabins; he could go and speak to them there.

The owners were Joe and Jocelyn Watmuff. I had arrived at the trading post earlier in the day, and sort of collapsed on their forecourt. 'Collapsed' is probably a little too strong a word for it: I arrived, stepped off my bike, slumped onto a picnic bench next to the vending machine by the shop, and immediately fell asleep.

After a little while, Jocelyn came out of the store with a glass of water and put it on the bench in front of me, asking if I was ok.

Her voice was kind. I told her I was ok but that I had been sick and was tired. She gently moved me along into one of their camping cabins and told me to sleep for as long as I needed. It was mid-morning and she kept an intermittent eye on me for the rest of the day. By early evening, when it came time for them to shut up shop, I already felt quite a lot better having had the rest I badly needed.

I had arrived at Swan Lake after riding south from Banff in Canada, along the long distance mountain bike route that follows the line of the North American Great Divide.

The Tour Divide is an annual race that follows the Great Divide mountain bike route, from Banff in Canada to the border of the USA and Mexico at Antelope Wells in New Mexico. This 2745-mile route follows as much as possible the natural line formed by the watersheds of the Pacific and Atlantic Oceans — the Continental Divide. The route crosses remote wilderness places and is truly a journey through the Wild West.

To me the Tour Divide seemed like the perfect next great challenge, a perfect blend of adventure, difficulty and beauty. I had been watching the race from a distance for some years, and had friends who had ridden it, some more than once. I had read about it, talked about it, dreamed about it, become a bit obsessed by it.

I wanted to go and ride it, to experience the place and to ride the length of the USA following the natural and romantic line formed by the Continental Divide. In some ways I was hoping it would be my last big challenge — afterwards I would not stop pushing myself physically, but I was hoping the urge to find harder and harder things by which to test myself would begin to wane. I think Aidan understood this. While at first he was entirely against me going — the inherent dangers of me riding alone over such a long distance, such a long way from him back home were foremost in his mind — in time he realised that I was quite determined to go. I think there was a silent understanding between us that this would be it; success or failure, my toughest and final big challenge. After that where could I go? I would not retire but I would not keep looking for harder things against which to test myself physically.

The race starts from Banff each year in the middle of June. I began my preparation for it in October 2009, the year before I planned to ride. I submitted a request at work for five weeks of extended and unpaid leave the following summer and it was approved. I set about doing more research into the race, finding out how to prepare myself as best as possible.

One thing I have learned over the years is that in races you can make your own luck, particularly in races where you are at least partially reliant on equipment for success. It pains me to admit this, as I prefer spontaneity and this sounds pretty regimented, but good planning and preparation pay dividends. You can obviously never account for the randomness of chance, but there are elements you can control within limits — you could write a PhD about this — that can make things easier, or at least don't make an already daunting prospect any harder than it needs to be. For the Tour Divide and bike racing in general I think the most important of these elements are your fitness, your bike and other equipment, your knowledge of the given race, and your wider experience.

As long as they are possible to achieve, controlling known challenges is relatively easy. I'm not saying that achieving them is necessarily all that easy, but that controlling the unknown — the not previously experienced and not expected — is harder. That's where problem solving comes to the fore and the most is learned. As you build experience of encountering, overcoming and achieving these unknown challenges, confidence grows. While it is important not to misplace this confidence and become arrogant, this wider experience of previous problems solved is an asset that should be valued; it can make the difference between success and failure.

I had learned this over the previous years of racing, mostly through my mistakes, and I knew that my preparation for the Tour Divide would play a large part in whether or not I got to Antelope Wells. As the race is entirely self-supported — riders must carry all of their food, drink, sleeping bag and other such gear — the bags I used to pack up and strap my kit to the bike would be so important. So-called 'bike-packing' bags are currently pretty specialist. I did some internet research and placed an order with a guy called Eric from Alaska for one of his big saddle bags and handlebar bag-strap set-ups. With over a three month waiting list I was glad I placed the order in December.

Much of the lightweight equipment that I needed I already owned as it was either required or useful for other races. Heavy kit slows you down in mountain marathons and over the years I had built up an array of equipment that meant my rucksack was as light as practically possible.

I wanted my equipment to be light — as light as it could be while still being of sufficient quality and robustness to last the course. 2745 miles is a long way to ride and progress would not be helped by gear failure. At the same time I had some sense of ethics and aesthetics and the way I wanted to approach the race was important to me. I wanted to do things simply; to be reliant on myself — my body and my mind — as much as possible, to avoid using tools such as a GPS to tell me the way. This would remove some of the key parts of the challenge: I wanted to find the way myself using a good old map and, as and when required, compass.

The race gave me a reason to buy another bike (do cyclists ever really need another 'reason'?). In recent years the popularity of the 29-inch wheel mountain bike has grown. Mountain bikes normally have 26-inch diameter wheels, but the larger diameter of the 29er is thought to be advantageous to the kind of long-distance riding found on the Tour Divide — they are 'high-rolling' and help the rider to cover these distances more efficiently than on a smaller-wheeled bike.

Sticking with my principles of simplicity, and no doubt also reflecting my stubbornness, I wanted this bike to be singlespeed.

Singlespeed means just that — just one gear, whether cycling uphill, downhill or on the flat. This may sound daft — what is the point in having a bike with only one gear? It essentially means that most of time you ride the bike, you are making a compromise in the gear ratio most suited to the terrain and gradient you are riding. The climbs will be tougher in that the ratio will be too low and you will grind uphill. The flats and descents will be frustrating as you spin away in a ratio too easy for getting up to and maintaining an optimum rolling speed.

Singlespeeding is all of these things, but it is also a whole lot of fun. Surprisingly, one gear can cover many different riding scenarios, and the simplicity of its riding is an attraction in itself — there is less (i.e. no) thought given to the gear best-suited to the situation, which means more time for thinking about other things. It frees your mind. If this is the mental side of the simplicity of singlespeeding, the physical simplicity is a big attraction too. Singlespeeding renders almost all of the bicycle's drivetrain — derailleurs, gear shifters and cables, other chainrings and cassette other than the freewheel — superfluous. The bike is both lighter and simpler, with less things to break and go wrong.

This simplicity was an attraction for the Tour Divide; it's a long way to ride and the less parts that could break the better. Riding the race singlespeed was also an attraction for me in that, much like using a map and compass instead of a GPS, the focus, and whether I was to succeed or fail, was shifted away from my equipment on to myself. I think subconsciously this was one of my main motivations. In attempting to singlespeed the Tour Divide I was not trying to set a precedent — a number of riders had successfully done so previously — I was trying to ride it on my own terms, following rules unwritten by me but which would mean I could wholly recognise the achievement, as and when I achieved it.

Having decided to ride the race singlespeed, I set about planning the build of the bike. What parts would give the perfect blend of strength, longevity and light weight that together would form my ideal ride for the Tour Divide?

I started with the frame. Bicycle frames can be made from a number of different materials: aluminium, carbon fibre, steel, titanium. Each has a number of different proprietary blends unique to the manufacturer, and each material has its benefits and otherwise. Some of these benefits are obvious — weight, strength, durability — while others only become clear when you ride the bike built around the given frame. The feel of the ride is important to many cyclists, and each of these materials has a feel of its own.

When choosing which bike to buy and to ride, aside from expense (which to a large extent governs the frame material) any cyclist who is aware of, and who cares enough about the effects of these different materials, will need to choose between them. I could write at considerable length about this and my experience of riding different frames, but, in summary, aluminium is stiff and responsive, carbon fibre is light and compliant. Steel and titanium are similar in some ways in that they both offer a twangy, comfortable and yet assured fast ride. In terms of longevity a well-built titanium frame will last the rider a lifetime. With care and occasional paint re-sprays a steel frame could do the same. An aluminium frame will last a long time but will fatigue.

Over the years I have owned and ridden bikes made from all four materials, and I have very much enjoyed riding each one of them. The memory of the ride of some bikes has stayed with me — that 'just right' feel that allows you to get the best out of your abilities as a rider. One of these was the carbon fibre road bike I crashed on the Isle of Harris: it unfortunately cracked in two. Another was one of my first mountain bikes — an aluminium framed bike that I had bought to replace the steel one destroyed when I and it got hit by a car. I rode it and rode it, I loved the way I could throw it around while going downhill, pushing the limits of my descending abilities and yet always feeling in control. I eventually sold it to a friend and happily it still lives on, hitting trails regularly, enabling fun riding.

If I had to choose at that point my favourite bike ever it would have been the 26-inch bike I was replacing to ride the Tour Divide — my day-glow pink steel singlespeed. I had built it myself a few years previously — the frame itself was a steal, and a present to myself for my 29th birthday. Pink really isn't my colour, but the irony of that, and probably my subconscious handling my concern over the fact that I was soon to turn 30 by getting something that was far from grown-up, appealed to me. The frame's steel tubes were made from Reynolds 853 — classic and renowned. Its geometry made it great to climb and descend on and it rode brilliantly through swoopy singletrack. I loved riding around my local Chevin trails on it and riding it further afield, into the Dales and beyond, to other adventures. While in many ways I would be sorry to replace it, I found the anticipation of building the new bike exciting.

There was no doubt in my mind that the frame that would replace my day-glow pink singlespeed should be made of steel. Steel has a greater heritage than the other choices I could have made, it was the material from which the frames of those great early-day riders — the first protagonists of the grand tours and one-day spring classics — were constructed and ridden to such glorious success and failure. It has a certain twang to it, despite its rigidity it has a suppleness that I can't quite describe or place; it helps you to feel part of the ride, probably because the nature of steel is that it is compliant, it absorbs and therefore softens some of the harshness of the terrain being ridden.

While the majority of steel frames on the market today are mass-produced in the far East, some are still handbuilt to exacting standards, by craftspeople who love their trade and love to ride their bikes. A frame built in this way is bespoke to the rider. I hankered after a frame built by someone who I knew loved to ride, and who loved the beauty and utility of the bicycle.

I met Ira Ryan at the Cent Cols challenge in the Alps. A talented cyclist, Ira also struck me as thoughtful and kind and, rather like everyone along for the ride of the Cent Cols, someone who truly loved riding a bike. Shortly after returning home I was flicking through a cycling journal when I saw a photo of him holding an unpainted steel frame — Ira was a frame-builder, he made that!

Perhaps unsurprisingly for an American who loves cycling and mountainous places, Ira lives in Portland, Oregon, the cycling capital of the USA. He runs a small workshop: just him, his frames and a long waiting list of those who appreciate his thoughtful skills, and who were prepared to wait for him to be able to steadily work through his list until it was their turn. Patient people who believe and understand that there are some things which are worth the wait; any one of them could have gone with a cheaper mass-produced frame and received it in days rather than months or even years. The frame they were waiting for would last a lifetime of riding, and would have been built to entirely suit their needs, all by hand, by someone who loves to ride. The frame they were waiting for would have immense quality.

In the autumn of 2009 I sent Ira an email, explaining my plans for the next summer and my dream frame — a steel 29er singlespeed in bubblegum pink.

Ira and I shared memories of the Cent Cols and Ira figured that he would be able to squeeze in an additional frame build in late spring. That was kind of him. As someone who values all of his customers and truly cares about the quality of his work, it meant he would have to work more hours to build my frame. Time is precious to all of us. He feels the drive to ride his bike long miles too, and I think he wanted to help me to ride the Tour Divide the way I wanted to.

In late 2010 — a few months after my summer adventure in the USA — I watched a documentary that was all about bikes. It was presented by a writer called Robert Penn, and was based on his book — *It's all about the bike*. A play on words from Lance Armstrong's autobiography *It's not about the bike*, Penn's book is about his quest to build his own dream bike; his perfect machine.

Penn's dream is to have a road bike he can ride every day, for the rest of his life. It wasn't to be a racing bike, built with the superlight parts that help the rider to go faster, but that trade their longevity for their lightness. It was to be a bike constructed of quality parts that would stand the test of time. The resulting steed would still be light, but it would offer a solid, reliable ride, and would be built to last.

Penn started with the frame, which was steel and handbuilt in Stoke-on-Trent by renowned frame-builder Brian Rourke and his son Jason. His saddle was leather, a classic British-made Brooks, and his wheel hubs were Royce, a lesser-known brand but, to those in the know, another UK company that manufactures some of the best quality and most durable hubs around. Penn then started travelling further afield, to Italy for his Campagnolo groupset and handlebars, to the US for his Chris King headset and he had his wheels built by a dude in California.

Along the way he meets and rides with some of the aficionados of road cycling in Italy, and the original protagonists of mountain biking, the Repack riders of Marin County. He visits the cycle city that is Portland, Oregon and many other people and places, all of whom are different but all share a love of the bicycle and the places it takes them. At the end of his travels he has his dream bike, and probably more than enough material for the book, the writing of which must have at least in part inspired the journey.

Like many other cyclists I am sure, I recognised Penn's desire to find his perfect bike because I had felt it too. I understood his drive and zeal; in travelling the world visiting factories and fellow bike aficionados, Penn was paying homage to the machine he loved, which had taken him to so many different places. Beauty is in the eye of the beholder and each of us has our own tastes. I appreciated all of his choices but I do think he should have gone to Japan and got some solid Nitto handlebars and a matching quill stem rather than the carbon fibre Italian Cinelli ones he favoured!

Ira built me a beautiful frame and with help from my local bike shop

I sourced the parts that for me would make the bike both aesthetically and practically worthy of the task that lay ahead of it. Like Penn I had spent thousands of pounds on it, but I felt it was worth it: I had never got so close to my idea of a perfect bike.

FIFTEEN

PREPARATION

While I was preparing the physical equipment I would need to ride the Tour Divide, I was also training my body for it. Over the winter of 2009 and into the spring of 2010 my training stayed largely the same as usual: plenty of variety and long steady days out in the hills running and biking. Given that this was a hard winter, I also got some fantastic days ski-touring in the Yorkshire Dales and Scottish Highlands under my belt. Long days out like these have always given me the base I need for summer adventures and more importantly they are also a lot of fun. Speed work was helped by local night-time fell races around Wharfedale. There is a lot of satisfaction in blasting off the day at work by racing around trails and fells in the dark. It beats the gym every time.

Many veterans of the Tour Divide say 'the only way to train for the Divide is to ride the Divide'. What they mean is it is hard to replicate riding well over one hundred off-road miles each day for the 20 to 30 days it generally takes those who finish the race. It is unrelenting. Most riders work for a living and have families and another life back home; to try and replicate the challenge of the Tour Divide for an extended period would be difficult in so many ways.

The need to train both myself and to test my kit was the extra bit of inspiration I needed to go and do some rides I had been meaning to do for some time: the three 3-day trips cycling the coast-to-coasts of Wales,

Scotland and England. These had been on my to-do list for years, but I had kept putting them off to go racing instead. During these rides I would use the equipment I intended to take to America, and would test it in similar kinds of conditions to those I would find on the Divide. In themselves, these cycling journeys are classics. They traverse some of the finest British upland terrain; remote places that it is a joy to ride a bike across, climbing all of those hills and passes, whooping down the descents.

I started with Wales. On the Saturday morning of May Day weekend, a three-day weekend, I took an early train with my laden bike from Leeds to Conwy on the north coast of Wales near Llandudno. That day I cycled high trails across Snowdonia, from Conwy to Machynlleth in the far south of the National Park, edging the quieter mountains of Mid Wales.

From the coast I skirted the Carneddau on their eastern side, crossing the Ogwen valley to Capel Curig and then following a high path to slate quarries of Ffestiniog. Somehow I lost the trail when on the lonely fellside above these quarries close to the summit of Foel-fras. I cursed the tussocks as I pushed my bike over them: my pace had slowed considerably and I knew this meant I was all the more likely to finish in the dark.

From the Ffestiniog valley I rode to and through the forest of Coed y Brenin and then past Dolgellau and over the western flank of Cadair Idris, taking a meandering line towards Machynlleth. I don't think I will ever forget the view I had of Cadair as I rode south-west, heading for the ancient Ffordd Ddu — the old Black Road. The mountain rose up like a fortress, lined by tiers of steep crags, imposing and proud. I rode the length of the Ffordd Ddu into the quiet Dysynni Valley, and then took the high old-road over Nant Braich-y-rhiw, finally reaching Machynlleth well after dark.

I must have stood out like a sore thumb amongst the kids hanging around outside the burger bar and Spar store in the town centre, which together provided me with dinner for the evening and breakfast the following morning. A burger and chips at gone 10 p.m. is not really the ideal recovery meal for someone who has cycled for over ten hours and would be doing the same the following day, but it was all that was available at the time. I wondered how frequently I would find myself in a similar situation during the Tour Divide.

I had no tent with me, just a bivvy bag as it was lighter and smaller to pack down. The following morning in Machynlleth a mountain bike event was due to start — the Dyfi Enduro — which rode some of the best forest trails local to the town. I knew in the sports field out the back of the leisure centre hundreds of cyclists would be camping, and that's where I headed to sleep. While some people take things very seriously and race this Enduro, it has a very laid-back vibe, with a bar, and live bands playing in a big marquee the night before.

I set up my bed for the night close to the marquee under a large oak tree, relaxed and listened to the great music. It was close to midnight as I started to doze off, just as it began to rain; a proper test for the waterproofness of my bivvy bag. I stayed there a while, anticipating my sleeping bag would get more and more soggy. Happily it didn't. At around 2 a.m. when the bands had stopped playing and everyone had gone to bed I crept into a corner of the marquee to shelter from the rain.

In the morning a café opened up in the marquee, ran by the same people who had organized the previous night's bar. I supplemented my Spar-bought breakfast with mugs of tea and homemade flapjack. I headed south from Machynlleth on quiet roads that took me to a trail close to the summit of Foel Fadian. From there I followed a slow-going path — more tussocks — along a valley that runs along the side of Pen Pumlumon Fawr, and eventually to the forest of Nant-yr-Arian. Mid Wales is beautiful and so quiet; I passed through this amazing landscape alone.

After a cup of tea in the forest visitor centre, I carried on to Devil's Bridge, and then south on the road to Strata Florida. I had ridden the trail south from Strata Florida a few times before, and remembered the big pools that form when the river is high. I finished the trail rather wetter than I started it. From here I had a road ride to finish my second day at Llanwrtyd Wells. I climbed over the brilliant Devil's Staircase — a fine steep road with numerous hairpins in its climb and descent — and then span my legs along the steady descent down the lovely Esgair Irfon and eventually into town. I had decided to stay in a bed and breakfast (in the Tour Divide I intended to stay in motels whenever I got the chance), and spent the night in the wonderfully eccentric Neuadd Arms Hotel.

The morning after dawned a perfect May Day: bright sunshine and a light breeze. I was closer to Swansea than I had originally anticipated, and further west. I had planned to ride across the Brecon Beacons on my way to the coast but had decided at the café at Nant-yr-Arian that three days wasn't quite enough to fit them in and so changed my plan. I still had a good eight-hour ride to the Gower from Llanwrtyd Wells, following a winding route with as much off-road as possible to the coast. I had no time to linger before boarding the first of a series of trains that would take me home via Cardiff, the Welsh Marches, Shropshire, Manchester and finally Leeds, from where I cycled home to Otley, and then reversed the journey into the city the following morning for work.

The first of my three rides was done and I was happy. Not only had it been a fantastic route to follow, physically I had felt solid throughout. My Alaskan bike-packing kit had worked well and, while I was travelling light, I had begun to realise what kit I really needed and what was just nice to have. Comforts can help but they also slow you down.

The following weekend we headed to Scotland. Aidan came too — he planned to bag some Munros during the day and meet me in the evenings in the places where we were staying. We travelled up on the Friday after work, and I was looking forward to another three-day weekend.

I set off from Skye Bridge just outside Kyle of Lochalsh on the west coast on another perfect May morning. I followed the main road for just over ten miles, breaking off left just before the majestic Five Sisters of Kintail at the opening of Glen Shiel. I took a track along Gleann Lichd that climbed steeply at times up to the bealach at Cnoc Biodaig, the pass that linked this valley to that of Glen Affric.

I think this glen is one of the finest in the Highlands. There is a Youth Hostel about halfway along it, our stop for the first night. Remote as far as hostels go, this one has no road access and is popular with walkers for this fact, and for the hills it sits in the shelter of. This first day was the shortest of the three for me; I couldn't resist the temptation to get off my bike at the foot of Ciste Dhubh, swap my cycling shoes for the studded fell running shoes I had strapped to the top of my saddlebag, and do a quick out-and-back to the top of this hill. The view from the top was immense. I was in the middle of some fine mountain country and basked in it.

Looking to the Five Sisters of Kintail while riding the Scottish Coast-to-Coast in 2010.

The following morning, after a big bowl of porridge, I started riding just before seven. I headed down the glen, first south-east and then due south to the wide Glen Moriston on a good track that at its high-point passed Loch na Beinne Baine. A still morning, the mountains were reflected perfectly on Loch Affric as I cycled by. From this glen I had another climb over to Fort Augustus through the Inchnacardoch Forest, and then onto the big beast of the day, the Corrieyairack Pass.

Part of General Wade's old military road, the Corrieyairack is the highest pass of its kind in the Highlands and I think the UK, reaching a height of around 800 metres. A national historic monument, this old road was of great strategic importance in the era of General Wade, forming a direct connection between the mountains of Lochaber in the west and the Cairngorms in the east — each so different from the other in character but altogether so Scottish. Cycling this pass was a highlight of the whole ride, something I had wanted to do for years; a real classic with much associated history and natural beauty.

After a long and scenic climb from Fort Augustus I reached the top of the Corrieyairack at around 4 p.m., with plenty of hours of riding in my legs and still a few more to go. The bealach reminded me of high Alpine passes in its nature and feel, as did the descent, which was fast, rocky and long. From the foot of the pass on its southern side I had a long ride down a quiet road to the village of Kingussie in Glen Spey. A quick stop at the Co-op for a few provisions and I was off on the last leg of the day — from Kingussie I would ride into the Rothie-murchus Forest, cross into Glen Feshie and follow the river for a few miles to reach the Ruigh Aiteachain bothy.

The day was moving fast. It was well past 7 p.m. when I crossed the river and followed a path along its southern side, and almost 8 p.m. by the time the bothy came into view.

The sight of smoke rising from of the bothy's chimney was more than welcome. Aidan had arrived a few hours earlier and, after spending some time watching a barn owl, had got a fire going in the stove. After hanging my socks up to dry, I boiled-up a big plate of pasta and we shared stories of our day.

The following morning we overslept to 7 a.m., an hour past my planned 6 a.m. start time. I had another long day to come, around the Cairngorms to Braemar, through to Balmoral and over Mount Keen before a long stretch to the east coast and the town of Montrose. Thankfully the bothy was right on my route, and from it I followed the track that rises up Glen Feshie and circumnavigates the central Cairngorm massif.

The trail improved as I approached White Bridge a few miles from the Linn of Dee, one of the main access points to the southern Cairngorms. Despite being alone I felt a presence. A huge brown shape moved through my peripheral vison and over my head, its few sweeping wingbeats belying its power and grace. A golden eagle. Its sheer size and finger-like wingtips clearly distinguishing it from the smaller buzzard. I stopped still and marvelled as it followed the river south-west. For a time it glided around in the same area, perhaps spying its next victim. Much like the time I was running along Skye's Trotternish ridge, it felt special to see such an amazing creature in its own habitat, a Laird of the sky in this wild mountain place.

Figuring I still had between five and seven hours to ride before I got to Montrose, I stopped at the Co-op in Braemar for more food. From here I headed down Glen Dee, skirting past Balmoral castle and the Lochnagar range of hills. Mount Keen is a hill that sits on its own; it can be reached from Lochnagar by traversing high ground but it is far enough away to be disconnected and alone. It is the most easterly Munro, and my route took me directly over it, along the old Fungal road from Aboyne to drop down to the mountain's southern side, and the road that would take me to Montrose.

From the trig point of Mount Keen I dropped east down a rocky track to the Glen below. The sky had cleared, I had sunshine as my companion for the 25 miles or so I still had to ride through to Montrose.

It was early evening by then and I pushed hard on the pedals; from Montrose we still had to drive home to Otley before work the next day. I rolled into town at around 7 p.m.; Aidan met me by the seafront and took my photograph. It had been another amazing day, altogether the things I had seen and done, and the places I had been over those three days form special memories in my mind.

Two down, one to go.

Less than a week later I stood at St Bees Head on the west coast of Cumbria. It was another beautiful May morning, still early, with a cool edge to what was clearly going to become a hot day. I had originally planned to ride the English Coast-to-Coast, from St Bees to Robin Hood's Bay on the east coast. This route takes in some of the finest English national parks — the Lake District, Yorkshire Dales and North York Moors. For various reasons I only had two days to ride instead of the three I had originally hoped. Instead of the three-day ride to Robin Hood's Bay I would ride from St Bees, following the route of the coast-to-coast across the Lake District, and then take a diagonal line heading south-east across the Yorkshire Dales back home to Otley.

My ride across the Lake District covered many of the finest trails in this national park. During the first day I cycled up the long Ennerdale valley, carrying my bike over Black Sail Pass to Wasdale. From here I headed to Eskdale past Burnmoor tarn, and then crossed over to the Duddon Valley. I rode over the Walna Scar Road to Coniston, where I enjoyed a fish and chip supper before cycling along some of the trails that criss-cross the Tilberthwaite slate mines to Little Langdale. I couldn't resist a couple of pints in the pub; it had been a wonderful day and I felt like drinking its toast. As night fell I left the pub, cycling through to Elterwater where I would bivvy on the lower slopes of Silver Howe. It was a magical night sleeping in the shadow of the Langdale Pikes.

The following morning dawned calm, sunny and warm. The sunrise briefly embossed a pink hue on the very tops of Bowfell, Harrison

Stickle and Pike of Stickle; I watched for a while before packing up my bed for the night and starting my day.

I was on my bike just after 5 a.m. I followed a trail around Loughrigg fell and Rydal Water before passing through a sleepy Ambleside. I was heading for Kentmere, via Troutbeck and the Garburn Pass.

Dropping into the beautiful Kentmere valley from the Garburn Pass is one of the classic mountain bike rides of the Lake District. It was here I branched off from my original three-day coast-to-coast plan; instead of heading east and then north, to Longsleddale and the northern Pennines via the Gatescarth Pass, I turned south, towards the southern Howgills and the Yorkshire Dales.

There is another Borrowdale in Lakeland, that connects the far eastern Lake District to the edge of the Howgill Fells. I cycled along the bridleway that follows this quiet valley and under the M6 motorway that crosses the valley at its eastern end. By now I was well off the route of the coast-to-coast proper, which crosses into and along Swaledale in the very northern Yorkshire Dales, before reaching the Vale of York and then the North York Moors. I was heading south-east, and had much fine Dales upland to cross before arriving in upper Wharfedale, down which I would travel to reach Otley.

I followed the road that skirts the fells. The Howgills are some of my favourite hills — they lend themselves well to fell-running and I've had a fair few memorable outings there. From Sedbergh I rode to Dent; I always find it confusing that these two villages are in the county of Cumbria and also sit in the Yorkshire Dales National Park. I left Dent on the track that climbs steeply over Blea Moor and leads to the Rib-blehead viaduct. I was in the heart of the Dales now — like the Lakes it has a character of its own that distinguishes its fells and valleys.

As I descended fast down the trail to Ribblehead I had a great many memories of the Three Peaks Cyclo-Cross race which also descends this route. It was different today: I wasn't in such a hurry and could soak up the scenery around me as well as that immediately before my front wheel.

From Ribblehead I crossed into Wharfedale via Birkwith Moor and Langstrothdale. The dry weather had made the trails hard and fast under wheel. I made good progress, enjoying being in such a fine place on such a beautiful day in May. It was good to be local again. The trails and roads of Wharfedale are very familiar to me, so much so that sometimes I think I take them for granted. Just because they are on my doorstep does not make them any less special; in many ways that makes them more so.

It was early evening when I arrived home. It was kind of funny; I felt like I had ended a challenge, something I did not consciously know I had wanted to do, but riding across and around some of the finest mountains in Britain had showed me something that was always there in my subconscious, waiting to be found. I had seen these mountains in some of their finest conditions, vibrant and gorgeous in the virile month of May.

While these rides were an attempt to prepare myself for my trip to America and the Tour Divide, they were each incredible adventures in their own right. Granted, I hadn't quite cycled all of the three coast-to-coasts (it leaves me England to do some other day, something to look forward to), but each ride had been amazing in their nature, and each of them unique to the country I was cycling across.

A large package was waiting for me at home — my frame had arrived from Ira. Over the next few days I built up my new bike and bedded it in with a few more long rides. I didn't have long to wait before I would fly to Calgary and begin my next adventure.

SIXTEEN

TOUR DIVIDE

On the 19th June 2010 I arrived at Manchester airport with my carefully-packed bike and everything I would carry with me on the Tour Divide. Aidan helped me get to the check-in desk with my luggage; when he left me shortly after, he walked away towards the car park and didn't look back. I watched him go with a sadness I had known for a long time I would feel but still hadn't been able to fully prepare myself for. It would be a long time and a long journey before I would see him again. My destination; Calgary, Canada.

About 60 miles east of Banff, Calgary sits on the final stretches of the Canadian plain, before the Rocky Mountains rise up to the Continental Divide. This was the first time I had travelled outside of Europe which was strange in itself.

I suppose I was nervous.

Although I had grown up watching American TV and films, and reading American books and magazines, and I would obviously have no problems being understood in another English-speaking country, I still an underlying nervousness. While I was heading somewhere I thought I knew, this knowledge did not ease my anxiety.

Furthermore, I did not always like what I saw. Canada seemed quite a liberal place, but the US of the media seemed repressive, insular. I combined this with brash consumerist behaviours, a society largely built on a strange mixture of Christian and materialistic values combined with a determined gun culture, and I ended up feeling like I would not want to know the 'average American'. There seemed to be so many paradoxes and hypocrisy. I had these feelings of unease despite knowing many people from the US, all of whom were quite different from the caricature in my mind.

So why was I going?

After years of pushing myself physically harder and harder, the Tour Divide seemed like the next logical step, the next challenge that could test me, enable me to explore my self when in an extreme place. I mean extreme in its literal sense — of a character or kind farthest removed from the ordinary or average — and not in the context of 'extreme sport'. I was not going to jump off a cliff with a parachute on my back for escapism. I was going on a journey, and intended to cycle for around 120 off-road miles a day, largely by myself, surrounded by the beauty and intense grandeur of the Rocky Mountains. I was 'going West', heading back to somewhere more natural. This journey would push me in many different ways, some of which I could see coming, others that I would learn along the way.

That the Tour Divide is a race also meant something to me — to test myself against others has often been a part of the challenge; to show what I can do an important aspect of why I race. As with mountain marathons and other races and challenges, it was important to me how I did it. By riding singlespeed for example I would follow the principles of simplicity and practicality I valued so much.

I had built my perfect bike and collected a multitude of lightweight and robust equipment. I had trained, ridden many miles over many hills all over the UK. I had experience of long distance cycling built up over many years of riding bikes. I had packed up my bike and equipment into a big cardboard box, carefully padded on the inside in the anticipation of rough handling while in freight.

I was ready for this.

I landed in Calgary to my first experience of jet-lag, dazed by the fact that it was daylight when it should have been dark. My big box arrived with me, more or less in one piece, as were more importantly its contents. In the luggage hall I re-built my bike; I had taken much of it apart to ensure it packed down small and to minimise the risk of damage in transit. I cycled out of the airport and headed west for Banff.

Riding to Banff the first thing that struck me was just how big everything was. Canada was on a different scale compared to anything I had seen before; the plain stretched as far as I could see in every direction except west, where instead the mountains reared dramatically upwards. My tiredness compounded this feeling of expanse around me, and somehow dulled the colours of my surroundings. Everything began to feel monochrome apart from the grassy plain that held on to a green tinge within its greyness.

As I got closer to the Rockies I was struck by how different they looked to the Alps — my only point of reference before I arrived in Canada. I can't really place what felt different about them — they were tall and jagged and snow-topped just like in Europe, but they did not have the same feel.

I arrived in Banff and headed to the YMCA. This offered some of the cheapest accommodation in town and — no coincidence — it was where many other Tour Divide riders would gather and stay before the grand depart. I shelled out extra for my own room instead of the shared dorm, needing to catch up with sleep. It took me three or four days to get over the jet-lag; I would stare at the walls wide awake at three in the morning wondering what the hell was going on.

I had five days until the start of the race, and spent the time wandering around Banff, eating, riding along the start of the race route from the trailhead out the back of the Banff Springs hotel, eating, bike fettling, reading, thinking (a bit too much) and eating some more. Throughout the week other riders started to arrive at the YMCA. It was great to meet them, to chat with them over a beer or coffee about their preparation and expectations. One of the things we talked about was bears.

Bears were another of my North American Great Unknowns, I had never had to contend with animals that have the capability to attack and seriously harm me out in the mountains before — the deer and grey squirrels out on the Chevin above Otley don't really compare to a big hungry Grizzly.

There seemed to be two distinct schools of thought on handling the risk posed by bears in the hills. The first was that it was highly unlikely that you would surprise a bear enough for it to attack you; it would perhaps be wise to ride with a little tinkling 'bear bell' attached to your bike, or a whistle, sing from time to time, and to be cautious when descending at speed around corners as bears are most likely to attack when surprise makes them feel threatened. This theory is based on the assumption that bears really don't want any hassle, that they will go out of their way to avoid people, and so making a noise to let them know you are there should be enough to keep out of their way.

The second theory was that bears mean business; they will go out of their way to get you, and it is necessary to carry a big can of bear (pepper) spray at all times with which to defend yourself.

It was clear from everyone I spoke to that, when sleeping in the open, it was necessary to keep a distance from any food you carried; ideally it should be hung from a tree if you wanted it to remain intact from inquisitive and hungry paws while you slept. There were quite a few other things you could do that would minimise the chances of coming head on with a bear. The most obvious, and the one suggested to me by a park ranger in the National Park Information Centre in Banff, was to not head into the hills in the first place. I thought that rather missed the point.

I think there were also a lot of 'bear stories' — tales with some underlying truth to them but that over the years had been at least a little embellished by the storytellers for added entertainment and fear inducement. Unfortunately my naivety in this area was so great I found it hard to tell which was based on fact and which was not.

The one thing I did know is that I really did not want to see a bear while I was in some lonesome place all by myself. Actually, I did want to see a bear, just from a safe distance, and I certainly did not want to surprise one.

After some deliberation I bought a whistle, a can of pepper spray and a bear bell, and started to wonder what songs I would sing to myself and my fears while out on the trail.

Most of the other riders who would start the Tour Divide — there were about 25 of us — were from North America. It was really great to meet and chat with them, to share our excitement, our worries and our hopes. I think the nature of the race and the fact that there is no entry fee or prizes means that those individuals attracted to doing it are not there for any material gain.

It became clear to me that 'riding the Divide' had an almost mythical status amongst many of those who mountain biked or had an interest in mountain biking over there. The route traced by the Great Divide must be one of the most obvious and natural challenges for a mountain biker. On a far smaller scale in the UK we have routes like the Sarn Helen — the old high Roman road that connected the north and south coasts of Wales — that crosses the Cambrian mountains and that still exists as a trail in some places. Like the Sarn Helen, the Divide is an obvious challenge. Rather like the natural line up a rock face, it is not at all contrived.

The days in Banff passed quick enough, it was soon time to start. At 8.30 a.m. on Friday 10th June, we all bunched together at the trailhead and the race began.

The trail was wide, and would be for most of the whole route. We all span along, and Matthew Lee — both the race organiser and Tour Divide record holder — was off the front from the start. For a race of this length it would pay to start steady, although ironically enough there was a pressure to eat through the miles during the first two days. On the second day I would be riding through the Flathead valley.

The Flathead valley is regarded in Canada as an extremely important area of wilderness. It is the last unsettled low-lying valley in the south of the country and is a haven for wild animals and is incredibly rich in all kinds of wildlife. A place to linger, to spend time appreciating the valley's beauty. However, a haven for wildlife means that it is a haven for the grizzly bear.

Friends from the UK who had ridden the Tour Divide before had specifically told me to aim hard to get through the Flathead in a day, that it would not be good to spend a night out there given all of the furry creatures that also spend nights out there. This was a widely held opinion of all the other racers too. It therefore made logistical sense to ride the 140 miles through to Sparwood on the first day, and then the 130 miles through the Flathead to the US border and the small town of Eureka the day after. This meant I needed to really push the distance on both the first and seconds days so, while I did not go all out from the start, I did not hang around either.

It was beautiful. The trail followed a wide valley along the Spray river, through to and over Elk Pass. The snow-topped mountains again looked like no mountains I had seen before. Wispy white clouds moved past their summits, set against the blueness of the sky. It had rained heavily in the early morning and there was now a refreshing coolness to the day.

I made steady progress towards Sparwood, sometimes riding with others, sometimes by myself. I knew that being surrounded by so many other riders was not something that would be usual, soon we would all space out and within a week or so there would be hundreds of miles between some individuals.

During the day I briefly stopped twice for more food and a break from the saddle, at the Elk Pass trailhead and in Elkford, about 90 miles in. It was getting dark when I cycled into Sparwood. Looking around for a place to stay I saw Eric and Shaun, two other riders. We resolved to try and find a motel room but eventually ended up sleeping outside a supermarket at the back of a car park. I slept fitfully, about four hours in all.

We were ready to go early the next morning. The three of us agreed to ride through the Flathead together; we figured staying together would be safer and would also ease each of our worries. Having stopped at a 24-hour garage to buy some food, we started up the road that would take us along to the mine that marked the opening of the valley. I was nervous and excited; the Flathead is one of Canada's last wilderness places and we were about to cycle through it. The sun was shining, I tried to forget about my nerves and enjoy the ride.

We stayed together throughout the valley, just riding along, telling each other a bit about our backgrounds and why we were doing what we were doing. Much like rock climbers, mountain bikers form a close-knit community — particularly those who ride long-distance tours. We were there for the adventure, the wilderness and the challenge.

A quick rest stop while cycling through the Flathead Valley with Shaun and Eric. Tour Divide 2011.

As Shaun pointed out, we were so lucky that we could even contemplate riding something like the Tour Divide. Quite apart from the logistics, we were fit, healthy and had the time and resources at our disposal to try to do something that, while superfluous to the necessities of our everyday lives, was something that each of us yearned to do.

The trail undulated and our route through the Flathead crossed three passes. We made steady progress and eventually reached a point where there was a faint singletrack trail about a mile long that connected two doubletrack trails and essentially made the journey into the Flathead feasible for the route of the Tour Divide. Matthew Lee had forged this trail a year or so before and this was the second time it had been used in the race. As we followed the singletrack, it steepened to a point where it was all we could do to push our bikes without falling over. It did not last long: we reached the next wide trail and continued to climb the hillside.

We had covered about 100 of the day's 130 miles and I was beginning to feel like we were in the home straight to Eureka when we reached the snowline. So early in the summer it should not have been surprising, but our progress slowed as we pushed up the deep and slushy snow trail. Shaun's weariness began to kick in and Eric pulled away from me. As we separated we each dug in to our own zone, pushing through the heavy snow. I finally crested the Galton pass; it was downhill now all the way to the USA.

I crossed the border at Port of Roosville without too much trouble — the border police knew about the Tour Divide so, after asking me a few questions, they took my fingerprints, stamped my passport and let me in to their country. Roosville was a small place, just the border really and a little diner. I ate some food and then planned on cycling the ten miles to Eureka where I would sleep. I found Eric in the diner. He had the same plan so we rode together. We got to Eureka late and, not able to find a motel, bivied just out of town.

That was how I arrived in Montana, home of the big skies.

The following morning dawned fine; we were again on our bikes early and off down the road. I rode with Eric for a few hours. About 30 miles in to the day's ride he pointed out a bear to me. About 20 metres away from the trail we were on and, with its head rummaging around in a bush, far more interested in its source of food than the two of us. I watched for a while and then got on my way; if all bear sightings were this benign it would be ok. Simply seeing a bear was enough to make my fears less mystic and more based in reality. I was still worried, but less so than before.

As we started a long slow descent after the Whitefish Divide that eventually took us to the town of Whitefish, Eric and I began to move apart. I reached Whitefish, it was hot in town. I bought fruit, chocolate, juice and a big pasta salad from a supermarket and sat down to eat the lot in a shady spot. Back on the bike, I passed through Columbia Falls and Swan River, and then slightly off route to the small town of Big Fork. It was late in the evening and getting dark. A trend was beginning to emerge: for the third night running I could not find a hotel and instead I headed to a bar for some food. It was here I found another Eric doing the ride, and we ate and then went to sleep by a roaring river on the other side of a bridge just out of town.

Three days in and I had done 400 miles. Too many perhaps — I was hoping to average about 120 miles a day — and certainly on not enough sleep. I had slept fitfully again and woke up in a despondent mood. I packed up my kit and started riding, leaving Eric who stayed in town to find some breakfast. I was on my own again, surrounded by a countryside that was beautiful but wholly unknown.

I think my tiredness compounded a feeling of loneliness I had been trying hard to ignore. It was only my fourth day of what would be around 25; I told myself that I needed to get a grip, to just get on with it. That was when the questions started — Why am I doing this? Why do I need to keep pushing myself like this? What is coming over the next mountainside?

I did not have the answers.

Why did I keep asking the questions?

I broke.

I stopped cycling and stood on the trail looking at the map. I put my head in my hands and cried. Why do I need to push it harder and harder and harder? The beauty found in riding the Divide is something. In the way I had chosen to do it, this beauty was not the only thing; wrapped up with it was fear, risk and fatigue. There was of course so much more than that but at the time that was all I could see ahead of me.

I collected myself and started riding again, continuing on towards Seeley Lake.

As I was spinning along a downhill I started to doze off. I tried to shake it out of me, keep the sleep away by singing at myself and to the bears, but it kept happening. I needed to stop for a break. I was at such a low point I did not know whether I would be able to bring myself to start riding again after this stop. I felt like I was cracking up. It happened so quickly. The day before I had been happy enough but now I felt so low.

Reflecting now, I feel embarrassed; it was only four days in and I had pretty much cracked. Part of it was the scale of what was ahead of me; I could rationalise, break it down into individual components that were easier to envisage completing, but nonetheless what I was attempting was big. There was no doubt that the lack of sleep was also messing with my mind. I remember the feelings I had — fear, uncertainty and a sense of desperation — and I knew these feelings would stay with me for the following three weeks. They would be interspaced with elation and wonderful experiences that I knew I would cherish, but that was not enough for me to be able to persuade myself to keep going. I already knew the challenge was over; I just wanted to go home.

I looked at the map and headed slightly off route to Swan Lake, where there was a store and somewhere to sleep marked on the map. When I arrived I stopped outside the Swan Lake Trading Post and sat on a bench next to a Coke vending machine. I put my head in my arms and fell asleep.

Some time later, one of the owners of the trading post came outside to check if I was ok, handing me a glass of water. I didn't say all that much only that I was tired. She introduced herself as Jocelyn, and suggested that I could sleep for a while in one of the cabins they ran on the ground behind the store. That sounded good, I followed her to one, curled up on a bunk and slept for hours.

Later in the day Jocelyn came back to tell me that she and her husband Joe were shutting up the store for the day, that I could just stay there and keep on sleeping and that there was a diner just along from the store where I could get some food later on.

And so that's when I met him. I was standing outside the store about half an hour after Joe and Jocelyn had closed for the day, gazing up at the sky and wondering where to go next, how to get back home. He rolled up on his bike looking tired and for somewhere to pitch his tent for the night, and asked me if he could camp on the ground behind the store. He looked like he could be doing the Tour Divide. I asked him if he was and got a firmly negative response.

His name was Rich. He was about 50 I'd say but he could have been five years either way. I introduced myself, and did not have to explain all that much about the Tour Divide; Rich himself had started it some years previously. He lived in Portland, Oregon, and had spent the previous six weeks cycling up to Montana through and around the mountains of the Midwest.

Rich was very proud of the bike he was riding. He had built it himself from parts he had found at the Portland bicycle co-operative, and it had cost him a grand total of $35. It had been good for over 1,500 miles and would surely be so for the same again, as he wound his way around the roads of the Rocky Mountains.

He put up his tent on some grassy ground around the corner from the camping chalets and went to check-in with Joe and Jocelyn. We had agreed to go to the diner just along from the store for some dinner.

Later, strolling over, admiring the calmness of the summer evening and the mountains, he started to tell me some more about when he rode the Divide.

He had quit the Tour Divide in Colorado, much farther along than I had got. He camped in his tent in the mountains by himself for days afterwards, trying to reconcile why he had done what he had done, why he had started the ride and why he had stopped. It sounded like he went a little crazy. I could understand that.

Nursing our beers we wondered why we felt it necessary to go and ride our bikes for thousands of miles, pushing ourselves in so many different ways. Is it an instinctive thing? A reaction to the unnatural nature of Western society — the sterile, ordered, collective entity that is a million miles away from nature, a million miles away from the environment that until recently we had to work so much harder to survive in? Is it a way of trying to stay sane as society forces us to live unnaturally?

Over the course of the few hours we spent at the diner we briefly found ourselves discussing madness. Both Rich's mum and his dad were reliant on anti-depressive and anti-psychotic drugs. Addicted to the stream of pills stored in the 'books': the plastic grids formed by taking the seven days of the week and the times of the day (waking, lunchtime, tea-time and just-before-bed) to give 28 sealed pockets, inside each of which sat a group of tablets, waiting like sweeties to be swallowed. I mentioned my dad, and at the same time we each realised; we did not have to explain this all that much to each other because we already knew, and that in front of each of us was someone who lives through and understands our fears.

Those books of pills haunted us both; to see parents reliant on them is both fearful and so very sad. Maybe that's why we were where we were, and why we had found each other. We didn't need to say anymore about it to one another, just shake our heads and smile wryly with shared understanding of our fears and determination. We clunked our beer glasses together and drank to the inner strength required not to be consumed by fear and anger, to stay positive through all the negativity you feel when you see a parent consumed by mania, psychosis.

Insanity is everywhere, in pushing ourselves physically and mentally sometimes we touch it. I don't think we should be afraid of this. At these extreme points we learn more about our own selves and our own abilities. But at these times we do need to remain aware of where we are, to retain a path back to places less extreme.

Sat in the bar with Rich, nursing my beer, Tom Watson's words echoed through my mind. Was this my ultimate failure? What would I find on the other side?

I knew I would not find that out straight away, it would take a while, perhaps a long time. At that moment however all I had was the desperate feeling of having majorly fucked up. I was a long way from home, from Aidan. Rich understood and wanted to help.

SEVENTEEN

GOING HOME

The morning after I had rolled into Swan Lake, I woke up in the little cabin at about 9 a.m. I wandered outside to the store. Rich was already out of his tent drinking coffee in the small café where Joe made supreme coffee using the real Italian machine that he was very proud of. I can get really anally retentive about good coffee — fortunately so could Joe. We had a heated agreement about the differences between a latte and a cappuccino. I told him that I could not find coffee finer than his anywhere back home. He asked me if that included London, and he was even prouder when I said it did.

In the diner the night before, Rich said that he'd cycle with me back to Calgary, where I would get a flight back home. We guessed we were about 250 miles away by road and so could do it in about three days. I have a friend — Henry — who lives in Calgary. I had phoned Aidan from the store, and Aidan had emailed Henry to let him know I was heading that way and to ask if we could stay with him when we got there.

We spent the next couple of days cycling across Montana, heading towards the Canadian border. The weather got worse but we got there ok. Henry had replied to tell Aidan he was in China but that it would be fine for us to stay in his house, sharing intricate details about where he hid the spare key.

I felt a relief that I made the decision to quit. There were no feelings of frustration or impatience at my culpability. I think I just accepted that I had seen a limit in myself and had decided not to move any closer towards it, let alone spend the next three weeks staring it in the face. I did not have to explain this to Rich; over those few days we wondered a fair amount about the things that drive us, that enable and impede us to reach goals. It got pretty philosophical and it was good to spend that time with someone who understood where I was coming from.

Maybe I was crazy to place so much trust in someone I hardly knew. I don't regret it. I learnt a lot from meeting Rich, about myself and about other people. Rich repaid my trust by treating me as I would have hoped, and as I believe he would have hoped someone would treat him. He did not have to go out of his way to help me — he did it because he could. I think we both recognized ourselves in each other — we both needed challenge to really feel alive and we both knew that in challenging yourself sometimes you fail.

When you understand that in other people, you don't need to say very much in order for them to appreciate how you are feeling and the help that you need. Rich immediately understood that I just wanted to get home. I was only in the USA for god's sake, not in the middle of some remote desert or wild Madagascan jungle — why was I so weak, so desperate to get home?

As we made our way to Calgary Rich began to discuss the principles by which he tried to live. He said that he could sum it all up with one word: utility. He strived to live simply. He ran a small decorating firm back in Portland, and the guys he employed back there were working on a few jobs while he left them to go cycling. It sounded like they had more than enough work. Rich had enough to enable him to live the life he chose, travelling as much as he could while maintaining a livelihood.

I think I thought subconsciously I was following the principles of utilitarianism. I wanted to keep it simple, maintain a purity to the challenge, to follow a certain ethos that could probably be summed up by two words: simplicity and solitude.

From the simplicity and utility point of view, I only had to look to Rich's bike to realise my contradiction. I have a beautiful bike that is unique, made for me. It rides like a dream. In reality though, all I did was consume. I spent thousands of pounds on an object that, while beautiful, in terms of utility it is the same as anything I could have got for a fraction of the cost. For this I would also have to forego much of the quality of my wonderful bike, and also accept that the bike I was instead riding was probably built and assembled in some factory in the Far East by someone with very low pay and bad working conditions, and who would be very unlikely to appreciate the drive I have to ride bikes. I would rather spend the money I earn on the bike built from a frame and parts designed and built by people who love to ride, who understand, whose livelihood is built around the thing they love to do. It would of course be a different story if I could not afford to hold true to these principles. I would either have to compromise or have no bike at all.

I suppose all I have to do is justify these principles to myself, but there does not seem to be too much long-term logic to the cheaper alternative. We keep being told by politicians and others that we live in a 'global economy'. While Western society's desire to buy products cheaply has so far been well served by the eastern tiger economies, we are slowly collectively waking up to the implications the associated loss of our manufacturing base will mean for us in the future. There's no such thing as a free lunch and it's likely we will live to regret our collective desire for too-cheap consumption.

In the mountain bike world riders who do not singlespeed have a general opinion of those who do. Beyond the 'why the hell do they do it', they are thought of as crazy but tough. Is that how I wanted others to perceive me? I love singlespeeding because it is simple and fun. Did I also ride a bike with only one gear because I cared about what others thought of me? Probably.

I told plenty of people what I was planning to do. I had a blog,

I was raising money for charity, I wanted others to know and to appreciate the amazing challenge I was taking on. I was building myself up, and I think underneath it all I knew I was building myself up to fail. Why? Because I need to have a ceiling, to know there is something I cannot reach?

Physically I could ride that trail. But mentally? Physical and mental fitness are two different things. It was easy enough to train to make sure my body was ready for it, but my mind failed at almost the first hurdle. Is my analysis an excuse for my failure? Maybe. But should I really care about that and what others think of me?

And what of the solitude. I got close enough to it to find a limit. Perhaps not the limit, but one that freaked me out enough to stop and step off the bike. This, largely constructed from a combination of fatigue, the unfamiliar terrain and place, the expanse of the landscape and my fear of the unknown — be it bears, cougars, wild dogs, hillbillies and all the other perils that lay in my overactive imagination — were enough for me to call it a day and hole up in Swan Lake until I had slept enough to start thinking clearly again.

Just under a year after my aborted trip to North America I read *The Monkey Wrench Gang* by Edward Abbey. Published in 1975, it is the story of four people from the US, each with quite different backgrounds, but who shared a love of wild places, an intense dislike for consumerist values and a hatred of the corporate machine that underpinned what they saw as the desecration of the American west in the name of industrial 'progress' — the bridge building, dam building (and therefore valley and gorge flooding) and everything else that destroyed and impeded on the wilderness, with the general purpose of ensuring the large natural resource companies with their friends in government could further strip the land of its assets.

Alongside his writing, Abbey worked as a ranger at a number of the USA's national parks. His writing combines a strong sense of revulsion at the behaviour of this all-American corporate machine with his clear and intense love for the wildness of the American West. Anarchistic and revolutionary in style, at the start of the book these four people meet and form the Monkey Wrench Gang. They then go about destroying the machinery, building sites and other infrastructure that supports the industry that they so distrust, the corporate steamroller that was steadily destroying their beloved wilderness.

The main hero — some would say anti-hero — of the Monkey Wrench Gang was an ex-Green Beret, Vietnam vet George Hayduke. Of the four members of the gang, the book follows his adventures and mis-adventures the most. It is surprisingly hard not to like this misogynistic, beer-swilling redneck: at his core is a deep love for wild open space, an intense hatred of the philosophies that he sees are going about destroying this open space, and a desire to go about stopping the agencies that embody these philosophies in the most anarchistic ways possible (always stopping just short of killing or harming anyone).

Throughout the book we are party to Hayduke's innermost thoughts, and it is here that some of Abbey's most lucid, beautiful and enlightened prose about the wonder and risk found the wilderness is found. Early in the story, as Hayduke is contemplating his satisfaction at the fact that he has the skills, knowledge and the minimalist equipment required to head into the backcountry and stay forever if he wanted to, we are treated to some of Abbey's understanding of the danger in doing so. He recognised and clearly felt the pull of wild places and the exhilaration of their freedom, but also recognised that in the deep solitude beyond this freedom lies madness.

I think I got a glimpse of what was there, and I did not want to get any closer. I ran away. The romantic ideal of wilderness, of self-reliance, journeying and returning to nature is underscored by the closeness that spending too much time with yourself in this wilderness leads you to insanity. It is a wonderful place but it is risky; spend too much time there and you could lose it. Some people can cope with this for the time it would take to ride the Tour Divide just fine. A few can take things further still, skiing across the Antarctic, sailing around the world, climbing unremittingly difficult mountaineering routes in the Greater Ranges. But me? It seemed not.

It would probably have helped if I had been more familiar with my surroundings. If I rode with someone else all the way it would have certainly be different. While riding almost 3000 miles and sleeping out in wild places with another person is no different physically to doing the same alone, isolation adds a whole new dimension to the challenge. The funny thing is that in my mind, in solitude is how it should be done.

In doing what I was doing I was at least beginning to behave obsessively. I don't think behaving obsessively is necessarily a harmful thing — most people who make breakthrough discoveries, all-consuming forms of art, wonderfully absorbing music scores are obsessed with what they do. So perhaps I was just thinking about it too much. Analysis of a situation can be a very useful thing to do but too much of it can be detrimental to the task in hand.

And what else did I learn?

At the beginning I was wholly ignorant of the US; its culture, its people, its history. It was naïve of me to form my opinion of the country from TV, newspapers and other mainstream media. All I really knew about the US was brash and materialistic, the crusade-like behaviours of George W. Bush and his cronies, and I allowed this to guide my beliefs.

My trip to North America led me to learn a little, and since then I have read more too. Mark Twain, Annie Proulx and David Bryne are just a few examples of the truly gifted artists and commentators that show much more about the USA, and what a mixed and varied country it really is. The introduction to the copy of *The Monkey Wrench Gang* that I read was written by Eric Schlosser; it seemed to mirror my thoughts:

'Mickey Mouse, Donald Duck, Barbie, Britney Spears, Ronald Reagan, Ronald McDonald, the Terminator, George W. Bush — viewed from overseas, American culture often seems like a series of extraordinary characters produced by some enormous, insidious machine. Linked by clever packaging and huge marketing budgets, they are predictable, inauthentic and hollow to the core.'

'But there's another American culture, dating back to the origins of the republic, that stands for an opposing set of values. It's a tradition of rebels and iconoclasts, of people who don't fit and don't follow, who won't smile and tell you to have a nice day. They're not cute, they don't think everything is okay, and they like to goad to irritate and provoke. Tom Paine set the standard for free-thinking, and without his Common Sense there'd be no USA today. John Brown and Kurt Cobain, Jack Kerouac and Abby Hoffman, Henry David Thoreau, Henry Miller and Malcolm X — they are just as American as the latest Disney cartoon or flag-waving Attorney General, yet they are fiery and passionate, embodying the spirit of rebellion.'

When we were sat in the diner at Swan Lake, Rich said something which echoed Schlosser's words; that he feels there are two kinds of USA — the one the world's media sees and the alternative one that in decades past has been characterised in some part by the Beat generation.

It's still there going strong, alive and kicking at the Establishment. Not all Americans are driven to consume but are driven to think for themselves, by being individuals, and it says much about my naivety, ignorance and incapacity to think with a more open mind that I had somehow assumed otherwise. Moreover, the kindness that people like Joe and Jocelyn showed me — the kindness of strangers — was everywhere. There were many people who didn't have to be kind or help me but they did so anyway, because they could. Ira squeezing another frame build into his jammed timetable — I may have being paying him but that wasn't the point, he sacrificed time he could have spent doing other things to help me get the bike I wanted to ride the Tour Divide.

There is a term — trailmagic — that refers to the kindness of others who don't know you but help you in a long distance journey in the outdoors. It may be giving you food, water, a place to sleep. It's a kind of altruism that is unlikely ever to bring any material reward but that pleases those who proffered the kindness in that they have helped another. In those few days I cycled the Tour Divide I experienced it quite a few times. The people sharing it are the kind that perhaps I should aspire to be more like; not doing something overtly for myself but doing something to help another because I can, and because it is the right thing to do.

Whatever I learned about myself, the Tour Divide — all of it; the preparation, the planning, the doing and the failing — confirmed to me something I already knew: I love the bicycle for where it takes me. Over the years I have ridden to all sorts of places, over all kinds of terrain. I have dreamed about bikes and riding, built bikes, wheels and plans, then headed out and ridden for miles; to, in and across wonderful places.

The rides to and from work are practical, they help to maintain my base fitness and avoid me sitting in a car for two hours, five days a week. More than that, they help me to relax before and after my day — it never ceases to amaze me just how many solutions to questions or issues come to me on my ride home, after I have perhaps been dwelling on them for hours in the office.

Rides in the mountains are one of the ways I choose to spend my free time. I go to special places and find calm. Cycling amongst them helps me to step back and reflect.

I love the simplicity of cycling, particularly when riding a bike with only one gear. It is so basic: don't think, just ride. This is further enhanced with a fixed wheel: your legs turn with the wheels — you cannot 'coast' or freewheel — if you stop pedalling the bike bucks like a rodeo horse and will throw you off. If this sounds intimidating I suppose it is.

Commuting through busy traffic on a fixie can be daunting, but only if you are not familiar with it. Contrasting with this intimidation, riding a fixed wheel really puts you at one with the bike; I find real pleasure in this kind of cycling.

Historically a fixed wheel bike was used as a winter training bike, something on which to get in all the long steady miles, the requisite base for a successful summer racing season. In the earlier days of racing, everyone rode fixed wheel bikes, in comparison to the ultra-light carbon fibre 22-speed bikes of today's peloton. Yesterday's racers were truly strong in both mind and body. The sheer brute strength and force of will they must have had to push themselves to scale mountain roads on just one gear. Given what these men put themselves through as they ground away, day in day out, in the Grand Tours, is it any wonder that doping became endemic, accepted within the culture of the racing cyclist, expected behaviour for the professional or promising amateur in order to scale the peaks and win? What a sad side effect of the pressure to earn money by winning, but it would be naive to say that it is not human nature.

Take racing out of cycling and what's left is utility, challenge and pleasure. Around the world, the vast majority of people who ride a bike do so to get somewhere, perhaps to work to earn their trade, to transport themselves and their goods, to visit family and friends. Most of these people ride a simple bike; it probably won't be fixed or singlespeed. It will have a few gears, brakes, a frame likely made of steel and perhaps it will have some sort of bag or basket attached to it. A bicycle serves its rider with a means of cheap travel that is more efficient than two feet. In the UK we are enjoying a cycling renaissance, in part due to the success of British cyclists on the world stage. It's also related to the state of our economy; when the chips are down and the pockets are empty, more people go by bike.

The challenge of cycling is exemplified by a long steep climb or a twisty, rocky descent. I can testify to the pleasure gained by cycling up mountain cols or down into a valley from the crest of a ridge. I do not need to be against the clock to find this pleasure — the mountain is challenge itself.

In riding the Tour Divide I was chasing. The win, the women's record, recognition, self-esteem. Surely my self-esteem should not be reliant on my ability to ride a bike for a month, no matter how great the journey. I realise I need to respect myself for who I am, not who I want to be, and I should not need my achievements to be recognised by others to feel content. This should come from within.

I was chasing for the wrong reasons. At the same time I was being pulled back home, remembering that I am not just responsible for my own happiness. My Achilles heel, my weakness, my love. Something and someone that means everything to me, I couldn't stop thinking about him, and I just wanted to get home.

As someone who works with and to a reasonable degree understands probability theory, I can sit and rationalise. The risk of anything bad happening to me is small, although the tiny voice in the back of my head kept whispering 'bad luck'. I was unlucky to ride off the road on Harris, to get hit by that car, to get caught in the avalanche when winter climbing on Ben Nevis, to fall off a statue while drunk at New Year, to fall off the scaffolding when I was nine, to trip over the curb on the pavement when I was two and a half. In honesty, all of these and more are a combination of bad luck and misadventure: chance variation made more likely by my urge to explore, achieve and learn.

I was sitting at my sofa back home, just over two weeks after the start of the Tour Divide, perusing a mountain bike internet forum when the title of a thread hit me:

'Dave Blumenthal RIP.'

I did not want to read the thread.

I had met Dave at the YMCA in Banff at five in the morning the day before the start of the Tour Divide. Like me he could not sleep, so we chatted for a while. He was from Vermont, probably in his late thirties and clearly looking forward to the coming adventure. He seemed so at ease with himself, smiling and calm, happy with where he was at. He spoke lovingly of his wife and four year old daughter, confiding in me that his wife was also the outdoor-type, and was jealous of what he was about to do. When I last saw him it was from a distance — we waved and smiled to each other as he set up his tarp and sleeping mat to sleep out by the Elk river about five miles out of Sparwood. Less than two weeks later Dave was descending a mountain road in Colorado at speed. He had a head-on collision with a truck and died from his injuries.

I feel uncomfortable writing about this, almost like a voyeur intruding on other people's grief. Dave died doing something he loved but that's surely not enough for those people who loved him. Many of us need mountainous challenges to truly be ourselves, to express ourselves. It is such a hard balance to strike. The reality is terrible things do happen, no matter how small the risks taken. I do not advocate never taking risks — far from it. It's just that I have found they have become emotionally harder to take. Cats may have nine lives but I really don't want to find out how many I've got.

I still dream about riding the Divide, cruising the trails of the Wild West. There are times I feel that nothing else matters but satisfying my desire for the freedom to travel across, to blend in with the amazing natural beauty found in wild places. At the same time I know that at least part of this is pure romanticism. The reality is harsher, tough to cope with and willing to throw things at you, to test you, to attempt to grind you down. I revel in the exhilaration of being in tested in this way — the point at which you are closest to breaking is the most exhilarating of all. However, there is far more to wild places than this thrill.

Later that summer, only a few weeks after returning from Calgary, I headed out to the Alps to run around the Tour de Mont Blanc. This is a fantastic long distance path that circumnavigates the Mont Blanc massif;

I did it in four days. I went to do this because I wanted to become absorbed in the mountains again. At the same time I wanted to revisit the reasons why I go to places like this. After my trip to North America I needed to revitalise. I found what I already knew — that there is so much more to that route than the physical challenge of its 105 miles. It was wonderful to run around it because it was beautiful and was there, not because of some race or another.

It was perhaps fitting that the book I carried with me to read in the evenings was *The Mountains of My Life* by the renowned Italian mountaineer Walter Bonatti — one of the greatest and most respected Alpinists. During a sixteen-year period of his life, in the 1950s and 60s, he climbed some of the most remarkable and visionary lines on mountain ranges around the world.

Bonatti didn't climb to win — most climbers don't — and found the concept of racing to be the first to achieve a summit or scale a rock face wholly distasteful. He climbed to challenge himself — his mind and his body — to explore and extend his own limits.

'Alpinism is more than just technique, more than speed records or a collection of summits. It isn't enough simply to attack a mountain, curiosity and contemplation are vital if we are to anticipate, feel and understand.'

By climbing in this way, he achieved remarkable feats while striving all the time to hold true to his values. Bonatti began — and ended — his years as a mountaineer keeping to these ethics, and at times found it very hard and distressing to climb with others whose values differed.

'The mountains taught me not to cheat, to be honest with myself. In one way, alpinism is a very hard school, at times it is merciless, but at least it is honest. It can be quite difficult to reconcile these lessons with the everyday world. You must strengthen your will, choose what you wish to be, then be strong enough not to succumb to temptation and change course.

You must pay a very high price to stay faithful to this agenda, but the spiritual legacy is in due proportion.'

Many of his greatest climbs were achieved solo — completely by himself with no climbing partner for physical or emotional support.

'Although distressing at times, solitude was an invaluable and often essential finishing school. I learned to know myself better as I made these internal voyages of discovery. But more than that, I came to understand others and the world around me.'

When it came to his beliefs in what was possible, Bonatti was years ahead of his time. His vision for what could be achieved in the Himalaya, solo, Alpine-style and without the assistance of bottled oxygen, was met with disbelief at the time but was later fulfilled by a following generation of talented mountaineers. Reading his book filled me with an awe and respect for his achievements, his values and his drive:

'In my heart I perceive ever more clearly that you cannot be given goals by anyone else.'

On the second night of the Tour de Mont Blanc I stayed in the Bonatti hut, high on the route above Courmayeur. From here I could gaze to the Mont Blanc Massif at some of the lines that absorbed Bonatti, and marvel at the incredible strength of mind he must have had to climb solo the wonderful and terrifying lines he describes in his book. The physical intensity must have been incredible and the mental challenge at least as great. Awestruck by his strength and tenacity, I could only imagine the places his mind must have gone to.

I have done a lot of thinking since the Tour Divide. I know I still need to challenge myself — sometimes intensely and sometimes I feel such frustration when I have not felt challenged for a while — but now, to paraphrase Bonatti, I know that I don't need to aim for goals other people have defined for me. I know where my true challenges lie, and, the more I learn, the more they become apparent to me, and increase in number. While these challenges are physical, they are also mental, and exist in so many different places — the mountains, mathematics, writing and art to name a few. At the same time I need to further value those things that are most important to me, and these things are not physical possessions. It's not just my own happiness that I look after. When we share love with another we take something from them and in turn give them the same part of ourselves to take care of.

I could become wholly obsessed with the Tour Divide; I have met people who are. The dreams I have about it will be with me for a long time. If I go back too soon I will fail for the same reasons. I will someday make these dreams again a reality — perhaps a long cycle-tour around the Rocky Mountains, maybe the Tour Divide — but I can't let myself become obsessed by it, it's not fair on those around me and there is so much more in life for me to do.

I find it so hard to accept failure, even though I know that without it it is hard to learn. I find it hard to leave unfinished business behind but there is more to life than reaming myself. It's still on the list, something to come back to, maybe in twenty years or so. Who knows where I'll be then but hopefully I'll still be up for a long bike ride.

I knew when I hugged Rich goodbye outside Henry's house in Calgary that it was unlikely I would see him again. He spoke about visiting the UK — something he had been meaning to do for years — and we exchanged email addresses but it was all a bit confused and I didn't get the right address. Spending those few days with him had been great, an experience in which I learned a lot. In so many ways he was similar to me, he spent time drifting, searching for something he couldn't quite place. I think he wanted me to learn from him; he had lost relationships in pursuit of his too often singular focus on some mountainous objective and he was a sadder person for it. In so many other ways he was full of positivity — for his children, grandchildren and his life to come. After his cycle trip he planned to move back to

Montana, closer to his family, to start up another decorating business and get by all the closer to the mountains. Perhaps he'd slow down a bit, although I think ageing was one thing he kept trying to move on from.

Why do I do it? I think I knew before writing a book that I would never wholly find this out. These days that doesn't bother me quite so much. I think through pushing myself and my limits, in both writing about them and exploring them, I have reached some conclusion and am calmer for it.

What I do know is that I must and will keep doing it. This drive has come to define me; through it I learn and stay balanced.

As ever, the next challenge is becoming clearer to me. I cannot wait.

Rich and Joe outside Joe's store in Swan Lake, 2011.

EPILOGUE

Chevin

How many times have I walked or run up this lane this year? I have not been counting. Johnny Lane is a steep road that climbs to the White House halfway up the Chevin. From here the road turns to a rocky track from which runs to some of the numerous paths and trods that riddle this forest and the open hillside on its top.

The day is only just breaking. Exhaling I can see my breath as I make my best attempt at running hard up the lane. In Otley it is cloudy, cold and misty; what will it be like at the top? I hope for bright sunshine but you never can tell until you get higher.

The trees are beginning to turn to their autumn colours, the track is muddy and sticky from rain, and the chill of October is in the air. Higher up the hill the mist in the trees begins to thin. Higher still I can see the sunlight beginning to burn off this low lying cloud. I smile to myself: it's going to be one of those morning runs.

On reaching the top, at the aptly named Surprise View, I squint in the bright sunlight. A sea of cloud covers the valley below; the Chevin and Ilkley Moor stick out like islands, as do Beamsley Beacon and Round Hill on the other side of Wharfedale. What a sight to start the day.

Although my day really started an hour or so ago.

Aidan is at home with our baby daughter. She takes after her mum in at least one way; she likes early starts. I am very appreciative of this time spent on the Chevin as these kind of runs are even more special now I cannot do them whenever I like. I value time I get to myself, and have an even stronger urge to use it in the best ways possible.

When I finished writing this book I started painting. A year later Alanna was born. It goes without saying that my life has changed hugely. She is beautiful. Now the three of us are a family I feel more complete. I think Aidan does too.

I leave the top of the Chevin, heading back into the forest and along the small broken path that follows a wall edge. Passing a steep-sided boulder I notice fresh chalk marks on a few pockets, a crimp or two and a sloping hold at the top. This boulder is hidden away, some distance from the rest of the climbing on the Chevin. I imagine the peaceful, absorbing time the climber must have had trying to solve this puzzle. Climbing, running, cycling, writing and now painting, they are each absorbing pastimes that can soothe as well as obsess me.

Painting mountains has helped me to reconcile the change of becoming a mother. I don't mean to sound ungrateful, I have a wonderful healthy and happy baby and am truly lucky, but there is no doubt of the scale of life change that comes with having a child to care for and to raise. I can no longer go running or cycling in the mountains whenever I like, for hours and hours, days and days even. Painting mountains has enabled me to spend time in them as my daughter sleeps upstairs, and this has helped me to stay balanced.

Painting has also helped me to see wild landscapes in a different way. I don't know if I ever wholly saw mountains as things to be conquered, more as entities that could challenge me, that could break me if I did not show them respect. Now through painting I see their beauty in enhanced ways, and appreciate their form and forever changing colours all the more for attempting to capture some of it on canvas. Like running up mountains, now I have started to paint them I don't think I will ever want to stop.

In the 18 months since I finished writing this book I have become a little more distanced from it, and this has helped me to consider it more objectively. I learned much from writing, and the experiences I wrote about.

I think consciously or otherwise I set out to find a limit to myself, to find a place where I would stop. In the Tour Divide I found one, a limit, and in that I found out a whole lot more about myself. What else did I learn from writing the book? That there is more to life than trying to do everything as fast and as hard as possible. I have recently had to slow down, and this would probably have been harder if I had not prepared myself for it.

Alanna was born in the spring. I didn't really think about it at the time because I was so tired, but I look back on the time spent outside with her in the early months, picnics in the summer, the walks on the Chevin and further afield in the Dales, as some of my most special.

As summer turned to autumn I started to feel that familiar urge. I ran the Three Shires race in mid-September with a huge smile on my face, taking it steady and enjoying every moment, even the last pull up Lingmoor. Watching the Three Peaks Cyclo-Cross come and go left me with more than a tinge of jealously at those riding. I won't stop racing. I don't yet know if I will be as driven to win, but the thrill and enjoyment of the challenge, the mountain environment and the friendliness of other competitors will keep me heading back. One thing I do know is that I will value these times all the more as I will be doing them less.

All too soon my maternity leave will finish and I will return to work; another big change to add to the many I have experienced over the last few years. The Tour Divide feels a million miles away now. These were formative moments in my life. Finishing this book marks a major change, but it does not mark an ending. Just a broadening of my horizons.

Descending the track back down towards Otley I pass the old White House and beyond it drop onto the path that is now lined with this year's old pine needles. Their rich orange colour offsets against the greens and browns of the surrounding trees and the ground, a simple contrast that for me sums up the beauty of the season. I run these trails over and over but they never stay the same, there is always something different for me to see and appreciate.

And that's just it. Time passes and things change but these places will always be here for me.

ACKNOWLEDGEMENTS

It took me almost three years to write this book. When I started I had no idea which way it or I would go. As I write these words some time has passed since I finished the first draft. There have been some changes with editing but I have always tried to stay true to its original contents. I think in this way it is a more honest reflection of my thoughts and the learning that took place as I wrote.

I have a few people to thank for the encouragement and comments that nudged me along to write something that was both publishable and that has the potential to be enjoyed by others. Shane Ohly, Mairi-Jane Mallen, Andrea Priestley, Sarah Fuller and Lou Brown provided me with this encouragement, as well as honest and constructive feedback that I found really useful. I think this book would still be in its draft form in the depths of my hard drive without their help. Thanks also to John Coefield at Vertebrate Publishing, who took this book on after we came across each other in a roundabout fashion. I must also thank Al Powell for his humbling foreword.

The last person I have to thank is my partner Aidan for his love and support over the years.

BIBLIOGRAPHY

The Prologue was first published as *Driven* in the second issue of *The Ride Journal*.

Material from *The Wild Places* and *Mountains of the Mind* by Robert MacFarlane, and from Sara Maitland's *A Book of Silence* is reprinted by kind permission of Granta Books.

Material from *The Beckoning Silence* by Joe Simpson, published by Jonathan Cape, is reprinted by permission of The Random House Group Limited.

Material from *Zen and the Art of Motorcycle Maintenance: An Inquiry into Values* by Robert M. Pirsig, published by The Bodley Head, is reprinted by permission of The Random House Group Limited.

Material from *Feet in the Clouds* by Richard Askwith, published by Aurum Press, is reprinted by permission of the publisher.

Material from *Dougal Haston: The Philosophy of Risk* by Jeff Connor, published by Canongate, is reprinted by permission of the publisher.

Material from *Kant: A Very Short Introduction* by Roger Scruton is reprinted by permission of Oxford University Press.

Material from *The Mountains of My Life* by Walter Bonatti is reprinted by kind permission Baldini Castoldi Dalai.

Approximately 178 words from the introduction of *The Monkey Wrench Gang* by Edward Abbey (Penguin Books, 1975). Copyright © Edward Abbey, 1975. Preface copyright © Robert Redford, 2004. Introduction copyright © Eric Schlosser, 2004. Reproduced by permission of Penguin Books Ltd.

Material from *Deep Play* by Paul Pritchard is reprinted by permission of Vertebrate Publishing.